THE LONGING FOR PARADISE

THE LONGING FOR PARADISE

Psychological Perspectives on an Archetype

Mario Jacoby

Translated from the German by Myron B. Gubitz

Sigo Press
Boston

 SIGO PRESS, 77 North Washington St., 201, Boston, Massachusetts 02114

Publisher and General Editor: Sisa Sternback-Scott
Associate Editor: Becky Goodman

Library of Congress Cataloging in Publication Data

Jacoby, Mario.
    The longing for paradise.

    Translation of: Sehnsucht nach dem Paradies.
    Bibliography: p. 217
    Includes index.
    1. Nostalgia. 2. Fall of man. 3. Bible. O.T.
Genesis II, 5–III, 24—Criticism, interpretation, etc.
4. Paradise. 5. Mother and child. 6. Jung, C.G.
(Carl Gustav), 1875–1961. I. Title.
BF575.N6J3213   1985   150.19'54   84-51937
ISBN 0-938434-21-7
ISBN 0-938434-20-9 (pbk.)

Cover Illustration: Detail from *Where do we come from? What are we? Where are we going?* by Paul Gauguin, courtesy of the Museum of Fine Arts, Boston.

Set in ITC Garamond Light
Printed in the United States of America

Contents

Part Two

A Psychological Interpretation of the Biblical Tale of Paradise and the Fall

Part Three

Paradise: The Hope of Future Redemption

Preface

The longing for freedom from conflict, suffering and deprivation is an eternal human dream of great emotional power. It is the
dream of total happiness, embodied in almost all cultures in the
myth of Paradise. By contrast, the psychotherapist and analyst are
confronted in their daily practice with an uncommon concentration of conflict and psychic suffering, which they sometimes ex-
acerbate due to shortcomings inherent in the analytical situation
itself. At the same time they must bear the burden of expectation
that it is within their power to free their patients from emotional
anguish. A "happy life" is often the anticipated outcome of analytical psychotherapy. The "longing for Paradise" is frequently
the more or less conscious motivation prompting people to begin,
and to persist with, an analysis. Symbolic of the goal of happiness,
"Paradise" is an archetypal, many-faceted phenomenon of deep
and varied significance.

This book, which was initially intended to focus on the
therapeutic process, attempts to circumambulate and reflect upon
some of the dimensions of that archetype. It is in the nature of
such primal, symbolic images that their psychic ramifications,
while constituting the very essence of psychotherapy, go far
beyond the confines of the therapist's consulting room. In trying
to study and trace those ramifications to some extent, the prac-
ticing analyst is therefore compelled to venture beyond the usual
limits of his professional competence into the realms of social
psychology, ethnology, the phenomenology of religion, theology,
anthropology, etc. This is one of the reasons why the present

work deals with highly diverse fields, some of which appear at first glance to have nothing to do with "the longing for Paradise."

A case in point is the relatively extensive commentary on diverse forms of maternal behavior, even embracing modern woman's struggle for emancipation. But those passages are in fact closely linked to the book's main theme, in that a mother's behavior has a decisive influence on whether her child's initial experiences savor more of "Paradise" or of "Hell." All the realms of thought that have been incorporated into this study, it seems to me, are related to personal or collective ideas of happiness and influence the various levels at which Paradise fantasies are experienced.

A certain minimum of religious history and theological information relating to the biblical tale of Paradise also has its place in these pages. In the German text of this book, all biblical quotes were drawn from the Zurich Bible as originally translated by the Swiss reformer Ulrich Zwingli. Since no English translation of the Zurich Bible is available, we have made use of the Revised Standard Version as found in the New Oxford Annotated Bible.

Observations drawn from my analytical practice have also been incorporated into this work, of course. I should like to thank those analysands who have given me permission to publish their dreams and other material. For purposes of discretion all personal details have been altered beyond recognition, while every effort has been made to focus clearly on the specifics of the problem under discussion.

Heartfelt thanks go to Dr. Sonja Marjasch and Dr. Ingrid Riedel for their valuable suggestions. Finally, I want to express my gratitude to the training candidates and auditors who attended my lectures at the C. G. Jung Institute, Zurich, and whose penetrating questions and discussion provided much stimulation for the improvement and expansion of this work.

Zurich/Zollikon, 1980

Introduction

The Phenomenon of Nostalgia

A wave of nostalgia for the past has been very much in evidence for a long time now and seems to be spreading. Antique shows blossom everywhere, with the flow of visitors apparently keeping pace with astronomically rising prices. Old dolls are popular —and incredibly expensive. Art Deco is in. Old farmhouses are at a premium as people try going back to Nature. And there is rising demand for old center-city apartments, to the delight of speculators and slumlords.

Sigi Widmer, historian and former Mayor of Zurich, has remarked: "Anyone attentively following the public discussion on city planning, the 'livable city' and the 'quality of life,' can hardly fail to notice that behind all the differences of opinion there is a common though nebulous image—that of the medieval city."[1]

What Widmer seems to be saying is that the longing for such cities, though vague and enriched by fantasies, plays an important role in our unconscious. It is certainly true in many European cities that apartments in old downtown neighborhoods, sometimes indeed dating from the Middle Ages, are being renovated,

[1]In an article in the weekly newspaper *Züri-Leu*, Zurich, July 1979.

equipped with modern amenities, and rented or sold at very up-to-date prices. Enterprising travel agencies are offering "the luxury of yesterday" on a resurrected Orient Express—with return trip from Istanbul by air. There are oldtime calendars and old postcards for sale at every flea market; even Grandpa's old rimless spectacles have regained their popularity, often serving as a status symbol for young people of the counterculture.

The same pervasive nostalgia is expressed in complaints of a very familiar kind: "Those were the good old days! People nowadays think of nothing but their own egotistic, materialistic goals . . . Young people today have lost all respect for their teachers . . . Nothing's sacred anymore . . . Nurses these days have no warmth, no joy in performing their bedside duties. In fact, all medicine is mechanized now. If it exists at all, a doctor's humanity is hidden behind a battery of complicated gadgets."

These are just a few examples of statements which imply that things were not only different but much better in former times. Nothing's the same as it was.

But were things really so much better back then? I must confess that, when I see pictures showing how teeth used to be extracted and limbs amputated without anesthesia, I completely lose sight of how romantic those Good Old Days were and feel very thankful for the medical progress of the twentieth century. No less abhorrent are the pictures of plague, pestilence, famine and poverty, of which the people of earlier times were helpless victims even in our relatively "civilized" latitudes.

Referring once again to the cities of the Middle Ages, Widmer writes: "Those who delight in the thought of how the medieval city seems to fulfill their modern nostalgic yearnings, should try to acquire a less unrealistic picture of what those cities were like. If they were to be suddenly transported back to such a place, most modern people would not only be horrified, they would perish wretchedly from a lack of physical and mental stamina. That is the reality."[2]

The reality referred to by Widmer was something like this: There were no sanitary facilities; garbage and bodily wastes were dumped into ditches between the houses and remained there until

[2]Ibid.

flushed away by the next rains. There was no central water supply. City dwellers lived with the constant companionship of chickens and pigs. Dungheaps piled up, enabling vermin of every variety to flourish, resulting in regularly recurring plagues in the face of which people were utterly helpless. Until well into the Late Middle Ages houses had no windows, since glass was a rare and expensive commodity. Instead, openings in the walls were boarded up for the winter. There was no street lighting, and people went to bed when darkness fell. As a rule, several people shared a bed, which was one way of fighting winter's cold. "Since the life of city people took place entirely behind walls, there was a spatial and mental confinement almost inconceivable by modern standards. Everyone knew everyone else. A truly individual life style was impossible."[3]

It is certainly important to be reminded of that medieval reality now and again. But, faced with today's traffic noise, it is still hard to avoid an occasional bout of nostalgia. At such moments we might do well to think of Schopenhauer, who complained of street noise made in his day by coachmen and their constant whip-cracking. He called that noise "the most impertinent of all interruptions, since it interrupts, indeed shatters, our very thoughts." And he added maliciously: "But, where there is nothing to interrupt, it is not likely to be much felt."

Back before World War II the writer Herman Hesse found the automotive traffic in the Ticino (Italian-speaking Switzerland) unbearable. By present-day standards it was certainly harmless enough; but to him, subjectively, it was apparently a great nuisance. Earlier, beginning at about the turn of the century, a wave of nostalgia had led many people to the paradisial landscape around Ascona, in the Ticino, where experiments were made with most of the life styles so much in the minds of young people today: anarchy, socialism, the promotion of creativity, women's liberation, communal living, nudism, free love, the breaking of the bourgeois taboos.

Through the medium of theosophy, the merging with transcendental reality was an important concern back then, precursor of modern pilgrimages to India, perhaps also forerunner of other

[3]Ibid.

"trips" undertaken via psychedelic drugs. At Monte Verità (the "Mountain of Truth," just above Ascona), which was still a paradise and virtually free of tourism in those days, nostalgia was already rampant. One of the leaders of the Ascona movement, the psychoanalyst Otto Gross, has been called in fact a "seeker after Paradise" in a recently published monograph.[4]

At a historically earlier time Jean-Jacques Rousseau suggested that mankind could find salvation only by going "back to Nature." The phrase became apocryphally associated with Rousseau, though it appears that he never actually used it. What he did write in his book *Émile* was: "Everything is good as it comes from the hands of the Creator; everything is degraded by the hands of man."[5] According to Rousseau there is also a state in which man is good and happy—that of the "noble savage."

Then there was the German idealism of the 18th century, in which Goethe's soul sought the "Land of the Greeks" and Winckelmann yearned for the "noble simplicity, the silent grandeur" of Attic art. Yet even in that selfsame Ancient Greece which was to be so sentimentally idealized in later centuries, there was already something like a feeling of nostalgia for a lost Golden Age when people had lived long and free of care, when there had been no war, no illness or poverty, when man had needed neither laws nor labor. This Golden Age is very like the Judeo-Christian concept of the Garden of Eden, the Paradise that was lost to mankind.

Ideas about Paradise are very widespread, going far beyond the Judeo-Christian cultural sphere. According to Mircea Eliade[6] the myth of Paradise is to be encountered virtually everywhere, in forms of varying complexity. The ultimate goal of nostalgic longing is a *condition*, then, a state of being which finds symbolic expression in the image of Paradise.

The fact is that we all tend to paint for ourselves a picture of the "good old days" that does not accord with the facts. There never were any good old days, there never was an "intact world." Surprisingly, this notion of a harmonious world which supposedly

---

[4]E. Hurwitz, *Otto Gross, Paradies-Sucher zwischen Freud und Jung* (Otto Gross, Paradise Seeker Between Freud and Jung). Zurich and Frankfurt: Suhrkamp, 1979.
[5]*Émile: Or, Education*. Totawa, New Jersey: Biblio Distribution Centre, 1972.
[6]*Myths, Dreams and Mysteries*. Harper Torchbooks. New York: Harper & Bros., 1960.

existed once upon a time is very much out of fashion these days, and people who still believe in it are regarded as bourgeois reactionaries who prefer to hide from reality. In our day creative artists can hardly permit themselves to portray harmony or wholeness in any medium. But that is all the more reason why there is a nostalgic need for such images today and why objects dating from the good old days are so popular.

The harmonious world which is now regarded as lost, then, never really existed. We project backward into the Golden Twenties, the Belle Epoque in Paris, the time of the *Wandervögel*, the medieval city, Classical Antiquity, or life "before the Fall." The world of wholeness exists mostly in retrospect, as a compensation for the threatened, fragmented world in which we live now. "How lovely it is to be a child!" can be uttered only by an adult who, looking backward, idealizes the alleged innocence and security of childhood. In their own way the conflicts and sufferings of childhood are subjectively at least as painful as the grave concerns of adulthood. But the world of wholeness, Paradise, is a concept which stubbornly persists in the face of all experience to the contrary. It speaks to a psychic need. So it must be taken seriously as a *psychic* reality, and may reveal a deeper meaning.

The word *nostalgia* means something very akin to the English *homesickness*, equivalent to the German *Heimweh*. The term comes from the Greek *nostos* (the return home) and *algos* (pain). In addition to homesickness in the narrower sense, nostalgia has come to mean a longing for what is past, a painful yearning for a time gone by.

To illustrate some psychological aspects of the phenomenon of nostalgia, it would seem appropriate at this point to cite examples from my own psychotherapeutic practice. These cases have been selected precisely because they depict relatively extreme situations:

Some years ago I treated a 30-year-old man who suffered from agoraphobia (fear of the outdoors, of open spaces). He lived in a boarding house, far from his parents who lived in Germany, and he could not leave his quarters without suffering the most intense anxiety. He needed the "security" of that house, as he repeatedly emphasized. *Geborgenheit* (security or shelteredness) was in fact his favorite word. At the same time he complained about being so confined and about the narrow, religious atmosphere of his rooming house. Initially I had to hold our therapy sessions in his room. Somewhat later, we would hold the sessions outdoors when the weather was fine; in my company he was able to leave the house, always taking along a straw hat to guard against "sunstroke." Gradually he dared to venture out alone, going farther and farther from the house, as long as he was sure that he could reach me by telephone from the outermost limits of his bold wanderings.

Before long he found himself able to come to my consulting room for therapy and even to undertake journeys, always telephoning from various stops along the route to assure himself that I was still "there" for him, a fact which gave him the strength to go on. At about this time he began to speak of how homesick he felt and expressed the wish to visit his parents. This meant a train journey abroad. Finally, driven by his mounting homesickness, he decided to undergo that test of courage. He called me once more from the Swiss frontier, and then remained with his parents for two weeks.

As might have been expected, his stay at home was a grave disappointment. There was a vast discrepancy between his fantasies and expectations of Home, Security, and all-embracing Mother Love, and the reality which he encountered there. Angered and disappointed by what he perceived as his parents' lack of understanding and icy unrelatedness, he returned with the firm determination never to go back again. But barely four weeks later his homesickness returned, and with it his desire to visit his family once more. The inner image of "Home" had regained its overwhelming power, nearly obliterating the sad reality he had experienced there so recently.

Another analysand, a 27-year-old woman, also suffered constantly from homesickness, could not remain in her own apartment and returned repeatedly to her parents, only to be disappointed and drawn into an argument.

Both these patients suffered from what modern psychological terminology calls an unresolved parental tie. But what tortured them was the longing, the painful yearning for something they had apparently never actually experienced: a home situation that would provide them with the sense of an unfragmented world, or what has been termed the "unitary reality."

The agoraphobic patient had been an unwanted child, born out of wedlock. His pseudo-religious parents had been forced to marry for his sake, a fact which had left them with a lasting resentment. The sense of *Geborgenheit* had always been notably lacking in his life. As to the young woman patient, she had experienced her mother as emotionally unstable, a religious zealot, very self-righteous, with little empathy for a child's emotional world. Nevertheless she recalled that as a small child she could never tolerate spatial separation from her mother and followed her everywhere like Mary's little lamb. As a result she often found herself being harshly rejected. Seemingly there was already a sense of "homesickness" at work in her psyche.

This homesickness or nostalgia is apparently related to something which need not exist in external reality. It is the longing for oneness with the mother in a state of problem-free containment, where total harmony, full accord, utter security and consolation reign supreme. Ultimately, it is a longing for the mother as the "containing world," as experienced in the best of circumstances in the so-called primal relationship, the initial link between mother and infant.

The perspective of depth psychology links ideas of Paradise, the Golden Age or the "intact world" with the pre-conscious state of infancy, when the ego as the center of human consciousness has not yet been activated. Erich Neumann termed this earliest, pre-ego period of the primal relationship "existence in the unitary reality,"[7] because at this stage in the infant's development there is not yet any polarization between internal and external, between subject and object, ego and self (in the Jungian sense of those terms). We will deal with these matters extensively in a later chapter.

To return to my two analysands: Neither of them had experienced enough of the "paradisial" phase of infancy. Hence they suffered from intense nostalgia and, despite all knowledge to the contrary, harbored the illusory expectation that *this* time their parents—and especially their mothers—would reveal themselves as the benevolent, nourishing, sheltering "world." Such hopes and expectations are based on inherent psychic dispositions, which exist as unconscious potentialities even

[7]*The Child*. New York: G. P. Putnam's Sons, for the C. G. Jung Foundation, 1973.

though they may not be based on actual experience. Those potentialities are expressions of what is known as the "autonomy of the
psyche."

The striving for the experience of Paradise as containment
within the "Great Round,"[8] the "unitary reality," is based on an
archetypal pattern necessary to human development. As an inner
image or expectation it lives on within us, creating a nostalgia the
intensity of which is in inverse proportion to the amount of external fulfillment encountered in the earliest phase of life. Despite
all the illusions and regressive tendencies it may entail, from the
psychotherapeutic standpoint it is important that the longing for
the positive aspect of the Maternal remain alive in the face of all
experience to the contrary. For that longing harbors within it the
yearning for confidence in some solid, nourishing ground. And,
at least in part, this yearning can be temporarily transferred to the
analyst in a therapeutically effective manner.

My agoraphobic analysand was eventually able to venture out
into the threatening expanses of the unsheltered world and its
alien railways because the mere idea of my existence—even at the
other end of the telephone line—gave him a certain sense of
security. It was striking to observe how he found himself able to
take that step forward only after I had given him permission to
call me at times other than those reserved for our therapy sessions.
In that case I took on the role of the "caring mother" quite concretely. By being permitted this regression, the patient gained
enough security to dare some independent undertakings, which
in turn gradually strengthened his self-confidence.

To repeat, I cite these examples from my practice only to illustrate certain psychic phenomena. They are not intended to buttress a one-sided hypothesis that "nostalgia" in every case derives
from disturbances of the early mother-child relationship. Admittedly, more or less serious disturbances of the primal relationship
are extremely common. But the truth is that separation, the "Fall"
from the initial Paradise of the unitary reality, is an essential aspect
of human experience and development. The crucial question is
whether this phenomenon leads to psychic maturation or, for
whatever reason, cannot be assimilated and therefore results in
emotional disturbances.

[8]Erich Neumann, *The Great Mother*. New York: Pantheon Books, for the Bollingen
Foundation, 1972.

You only long for something after being separated from it. The yearning begins after the loss of Paradise, of the mother or the loved one. *Le temps* must be *perdu* before the *recherche* can begin (harking back to the original title of Marcel Proust's classic literary undertaking, translated into English as *Remembrance of Things Past*).

In other words, what we have referred to as nostalgia is predicated on separation. I feel homesick only where and when I do not feel at home. In the cases we have briefly examined involving disturbances of the primal relationship, we observed intense yearning for the parents, mainly the mother. The remarkable thing about both these instances was that the emotion persisted despite the factual presence of the mother. From this it may be inferred that ultimately the longing was not directed at the real, personal mother, but rather at a mother of the inner world who does not exist, or no longer exists—and perhaps never did exist—in external reality. This is, at bottom, a longing for one's own well-being, which originally was dependent upon maternal care and protection, a longing to be cradled in a conflict-free unitary reality, which takes on symbolic form in the image of Paradise.

Ultimately, then, every form of longing is for the experience of one's own fulfillment, salvation, harmony—whatever you choose to call it—even though the manifest object of the longing may be the mother, the loved one, a tropical landscape, Holy India, bygone days, or what-have-you. In the best sense, the longing expresses a desire to overcome one's own self-alienation, to achieve consonance with one's own wholeness.

The phenomenon of nostalgia is initially regressive, of course, and remains so as long as its deeper meaning does not cross the threshold of awareness. Even regression, however, can mean a return to certain primal experiences, a retreat from the crotchety constraints and one-sidedness of rationality back to one's "own nature."

But a regressive wallowing in one's own *Weltschmerz* is not very productive in the long run, unless you happen to be a Romantic poet. It seems to me of decided importance that nostalgic longing not remain stuck exclusively in the concrete, in fantasies such as: "If I were only with my mother now, everything would be fine . . ." or "If only I could live on some Greek island,

surrounded by unspoiled nature, far from noise and pollution, I'd
be perfectly happy.'' Even the finest collection of antique fur-
niture, old dolls or out-of-print children's books cannot really
bring back those good old days—since what they stand for is not
so much a concrete, historical reality as a psychic reality. It is
therefore absolutely essential that they also be *experienced* as
psychic reality.

By way of contrast, in *The Sociology of Ideas of Paradise,*[9]
Alois Hahn puts forward the view that, as collective images of happiness, concepts of Paradise may embrace thoroughly concrete,
material goods of everyday life. He sees a connection between a
society's ideas of Paradise and its actual living conditions, which
is perfectly plausible. "For what someone perceives as the greatest
good depends on what he's already got."[10] According to this
view, the paradisial longings of people who live a harsh life in constant conflict with a threatening environment will be different
from the images of happiness developed by people who do not
suffer much from the threat of material need.

Hahn cites the Zunis, a Pueblo Indian tribe, whose concept of
Paradise is that the dead live under a great lake, where there is
always plenty of water. This is in direct contrast to Zuni reality,
which consists of life in the Mexican desert and a constant short-
age of water. In the Zuni afterlife, moreover, the departed spirits
dance and sing all day long. "But, for living Zunis, dancing and
singing are possible only on a few special holidays during the year.
The unusual situation in the everyday world becomes the normal
thing in Paradise."[11]

In general, Hahn continues, "the essence of paradisial joys for
simple societies or social groups experiencing external need is in
fact what constitutes normal, everyday reality for the upper social
classes of more advanced societies, for kings and princes, the
nobility and the high clergy. They do not need to long for bread
in Paradise, since they can enjoy it here in this world without any
effort on their part."[12] Thus the upper classes in more advanced

---

[9]*Soziologie der Paradiesvorstellungen* (The Sociology of Ideas of Paradise). Trier
University Addresses, Vol. 7, Trier: 1976.
[10]Ibid., p. 11.
[11]Ibid.
[12]Ibid., p. 34.

societies may no longer be concerned with external necessities and pleasures, but with the ultimate shallowness of pleasure itself.

In the modern welfare state most basic material needs are taken care of for nearly everyone, while in less-developed societies the satisfaction of those needs must be put off until the attainment of Paradise. Hahn concludes from this that when old concepts of Paradise are insistently retained in a modern welfare society, the process requires the "symbolic reworking of what were originally concrete, tangibly intended promises."[13] He sees the biblical image of the Garden of Eden, which bears its fruit without man's labor or effort, as the wish-fulfillment dream of a peasant farmer whose life is lived under quite different conditions. The image is, quite concretely, the embodiment of his wish. Through "symbolic reworking," however, to cite another biblical example, "the springs of cool water for which the people longed in the desert, and to which the divine shepherd led the flocks of a pastoral folk, [become] the symbol of the slaking of a thirst for inner peace . . . ."[14]

I disagree with Hahn's thesis to the extent that, from the psychological standpoint, there can be no question of "symbolic reworking." The psychological fact is that a symbolic dimension is inherently present in every idea, every image. To stay with Hahn's biblical example: Let us assume that the wanderers in the desert actually reach the springs of cool water. At the moment that their physical thirst is quenched, they feel a simultaneous sense of gratification, the momentary experience of inner peace. But as long as these people continue thirsting in the desert, their most urgent and immediate thought is: "If only we could find the springs, everything would be all right." Their entire yearning is for water, for without it no gratification can be attained. The image of the spring is the specific, concrete thing that is longed for—but at the same time it signifies an inner gratification.

Now, it is perfectly possible that a prosperous citizen of a modern, advanced society may dream at night about springs of cool water. Although he is neither hungry nor thirsty in the concrete, physical sense, unconsciously he would seem to feel a need

[13]Ibid.
[14]Ibid.

for something that is represented by the refreshing springs in his dream. He, too, is unsatisfied; it may be assumed that he feels psychically dried out and thirsts for "the water of life," the experience of the soul's vitality. In this case the symbolic dimension of the image is already in the foreground, without any need of "symbolic reworking."

It is noteworthy that, in this era of widespread prosperity, the predisposition to nostalgia always latent in the human psyche can take on the literal form of the wave of nostalgia referred to earlier. And since a society's images of paradisial bliss stand in a compensatory relationship to its actual living conditions, we are confronted with the fact that even our unprecedented levels of prosperity cannot provide true gratification or inner peace.

"Man does not live by bread alone" is more than biblical consolation for those people among whom bread is in short supply; it is not just the "opiate of the masses," as Marx suggested. Among other things, the thought expresses our malaise at our own culture, which has brought forth such an abundance of bread along with a vast array of consumer goods and tranquilizers. If a sense of nostalgic longing is nonetheless pandemic, the ideas of happiness linked to it are generally "not of this world"—at least, not of the world as we know it today. They may focus upon the "world of yesteryear" and everything meant and implied by "once upon a time." But most of all, they deal with the world as it could or should be.

Although I contend that nostalgia is ultimately a longing for a psychic rather than a historic reality, the more or less utopian concept of unspoiled nature should not be understood exclusively on the symbolic level (e.g., in relation to the naturalness within oneself). The concrete side of this image is of considerable importance, since it can provide the motivating power for the very necessary struggle against the increasing pollution and despoliation of our environment.

The image of unspoiled nature needs to be brought into reality in the here and now. Despite its utopian aspect and the apparent hopelessness of trying to realize such a goal, the image— and the psychic energy it generates—must not be depotentiated by a one-sided emphasis on the symbolic. There is much to be done in *this* world if a better world is to be brought into being.

At the same time, it is *also* true that nostalgic ideas of ultimate happiness are "not of this world"—for this world can never provide salvation, perfect harmony and freedom from conflict. Such images must be grasped symbolically. On that level, nostalgia, understood as homesickness in the terms we have discussed, means a longing and need to "come home" to selfhood from the foreign land of self-alienation.

Part Three of this book, which deals with ideas of Paradise as expectations of future salvation, will show that this idea of the Return bespeaks a psychic experience of great depth, including religious dimensions. Part Two attempts a psychological interpretation of the biblical myth of man's Fall and expulsion from the Garden of Eden, with special attention to the psychological meaning of the loss of Paradise and thus to the problem of the origins and meaning of man's sense of guilt. Part One deals primarily with the regressive longing for security in unity with the Maternal, and its many psychological consequences.

Through all of this we shall see how, whether oriented toward past or future, the target or goal-image of nostalgic longing is the elimination of suffering, conflict and malaise in an ultimate "unitary reality," which is graphically symbolized in the archetypal image of Paradise.

PART ONE

PARADISE AS AN IMAGE
OF PRIMAL BLISS

1. Paradise as an Image of Unitary Reality

Initially there was the closest relationship between Heaven and Earth. The god of Heaven and the goddess of Earth were husband and wife, or they simply coupled and reproduced as depicted in the Greek myth of Uranos and Gaia. In those cases where Heaven and Earth do not directly unite, they are brought into close contact via the *axis mundi*, the world axis which rises at the midpoint of the world and connects the two great cosmic realms. It is because of this connection that mythic man could so easily ascend to Heaven by climbing a tree, a ladder or a mountain, and that the gods could descend to Earth and move among men.

This imagery is widespread among such archaic peoples as the Australian Aborigines, Eskimos of the Arctic region, Pygmies, etc., and was commonplace among the great urban cultures of the ancient Orient.[1]

The story continues that, ever since Heaven was forcibly separated from Earth and moved off to a great distance, humanity has been in its present condition. The era of Paradise has come to an end. Separation of the "cosmic parents" was a violent business, involving castration of the god of Heaven (as in the myth of Uranos, Gaia and Kronos) or violent kicks (as in the Maori creation myth).[2] The tree or vine that linked Earth to Heaven has been severed, the mountain that reached up to touch the skies has been

[1]Mircea Eliade, *Myths, Dreams and Mysteries.* Harper Torchbooks, New York: Harper & Bros., 1960.
[2]Erich Neumann, *The Origins and History of Consciousness.* New York: Harper & Bros., for the Bollingen Foundation, 1962, p. 118.

leveled.[3] The break between the two realms is generally described as having been caused by an ethically dubious mythic event, which is nonetheless usually presented as necessary.

The characteristics of humanity in the paradisial state are almost universally enumerated as: immortality; spontaneity; freedom; the possibility of easily ascending to Heaven and meeting with the gods; friendship with the animals and knowledge of their language.[4] In a 1936 work on the subject, H. Baumann summarizes the African myths relating to the initial paradisial era as follows: "In the view of the natives, everything that happened in the primal age was different from today: people lived forever and never died; they understood the language of the animals and lived with creatures in peace; they knew no labor and had food in plenitude, the effortless gathering of which guaranteed them a life without care; there was no sexuality and no reproduction—in brief, they knew nothing of all those fundamental factors and attitudes which move people today."[5]

Immortality signifies no polarity between life and death, none of the much-lamented problems characteristic of life in the flow of time, with its dynamism of death and becoming. There is neither reproduction nor separation, since death does not come to sever the unity with the world and with other people. Moreover there is no conflict between men and the gods, only perfect harmony. "Visits" are exchanged and there is no sharp separation between the two realms. Unity with the animals is also an important aspect of the paradisial state. It is not difficult to empathize with what this must have meant to early humans, who had to be ever on the alert against attacks by wild beasts.

At the same time, this image of harmony with the animals, to the point of understanding their language, has a far-reaching symbolic dimension: Man is still in harmony with himself, not yet aware of a conflict between his own animal-instinctual nature and his divine-spiritual aspect. The possibility of effortlessly satisfying all need for food and fulfilling all desires symbolizes complete

[3]Eliade, *Myths, Dreams and Mysteries*.
[4]Ibid.
[5]H. Baumann, *Schöpfung und Urzeit des Menschen im Mythus der afrikanischen Völker* (Creation and the Primal Era of Mankind in the Mythology of African Peoples). Berlin: Reimer, 1936, pp. 267ff.

harmony between inner and outer. There is no discrepancy between the inner realm of wish-fulfillment images and the outer world of reality—this is precisely what makes it a "unitary reality."

But: Paradise has been lost. Even the most archaic peoples seem aware of that fact.

Ancient Greece cultivated the concept of a Golden Age which clearly evinced paradisial traits. Here is Hesiod's description of it:

> In the beginning, the immortals
> who have their homes on Olympos
> created the golden generation of mortal people.
> These lived in Kronos' time, when he
> was the king in heaven.
> They lived as if they were gods,
> their hearts free from all sorrow,
> by themselves, and without hard work or pain;
> no miserable
> old age came their way; their hands, their feet,
> did not alter.
> They took their pleasure in festivals,
> and lived without troubles.
> When they died, it was as if they fell asleep.
> All goods
> were theirs. The fruitful grainland
> yielded its harvest to them
> of its own accord; this was great and abundant,
> while they at their pleasure
> quietly looked after their works,
> in the midst of good things
> (prosperous in flocks, on friendly terms
> with the blessed immortals).[6]

The poet who wrote those lines lived about 700 B.C. in the countryside of Boeotia, by all accounts a farmer himself. This glowing image of earth's fertility and the wealth of livestock expresses the wishes of a people of farmers and herdsmen. At the same time the verses describe most of the traits common to depictions of Paradise—except immortality. According to Hesiod, death

[6]Hesiod, *Works and Days*, verses 110–120; translated by Richard Lattimore. Ann Arbor, Michigan: University of Michigan Press, 1959.

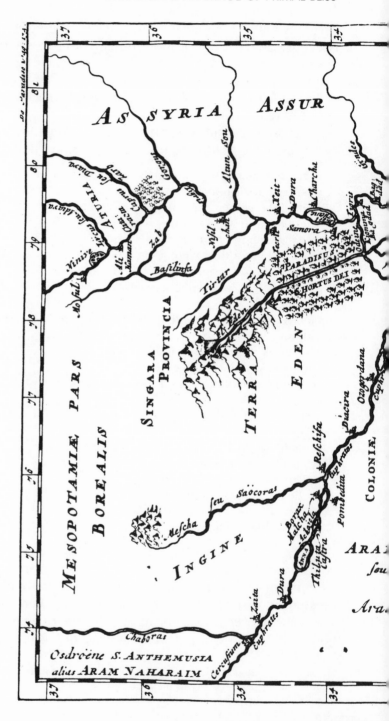

1. *The Location of Paradise.*
Kupferstich aus Salomon van Til (1701).

was already present in the Golden Age, but brought with it no suffering.

The Persians, too, had their traditional Paradise: the Garden of Yima, monarch of the Golden Age. It is situated on a mythical mountain from which flows the Water of Life, and full of magical trees, including the Tree of Life.[7] A Sumerian text likewise mentions the Tree of Life, as well as a Tree of Truth.[8] According to some of the prophets and later traditions of Judaism, the biblical Paradise was also situated on a mountain. Since that tale speaks of the Land of Four Rivers, two of which are designated as the Tigris and Euphrates, there has often been speculation that the Garden of Eden was actually located in the mountains of Armenia, where these two rivers have their source.

Very similar is the Indian idea of Mount Meru, situated at earth's North Pole. It has three peaks, upon which are the cities of the three divinities, Vishnu, Brahma and Siva. The Ganges, which flows from Vishnu's river, divides into four segments on Mount Meru and then plunges down to the lesser mountains below, The cosmology of the Babylonians and Assyrians also ascribed a central position to the World Mountain and the four quadrants of the world.[9]

The term Paradise, commonly used to designate the Old Testament's Garden of Eden, has its etymological root in the Avestan (Old Iranian) *pairi-daēza*, meaning "walled" or "enclosed." In Greek, *paradeisos* came to mean an enclosed zoological garden or a park; Xenophon and others used the word for the great park of the Persian kings. The word *pardes* in the Old Testament also means a treed garden or park.[10] The idea of a condition of bliss is thus expressed in the image of an enclosed garden full of plants, trees and animals. In the symbolic language of psychology this image can be expressed in terms of security or containment (the

---

[7]H. Gunkel, *Göttinger Handkommentar zum Alten Testament* (The Handy Göttingen Commentary to the Old Testament), 5th ed., Vol. I. Göttingen: 1922, pp. 36ff.

[8]Ibid., p. 8.

[9]See H. Bächtold-Stäubli, *Handwörterbuch des deutschen Aberglaubens* (Handbook of German Superstition). Berlin & Leipzig: de Gruyter, 1926–1942, under "Paradise."

[10]Ibid.

2. *The Earthly Paradise.*
   Nicolas de Bruyn (1571-1656).

3. *The Golden Age.*
   Nicolas de Bruyn (1571-1656).

enclosed space) in benevolent Nature (the trees), with instinctual-
animal needs (animals) being gratified without guilt or conflict.
From the tale in Genesis we learn that everything in the Garden
of Eden was pleasing, that there was harmony between man and
beast and that God lovingly provided for mankind's well-being.
Thus the biblical Paradise, psychologically speaking, may also be
seen as an archetypal image linked to the idea of a harmonious,
conflict-free existence.

2. Unitary Reality in the Primal Relationship Between Mother and Child

In the biblical myth, the paradisial state was lost when mankind acquired knowledge of good and evil, apparently against the will of God. Such knowledge represents the beginning of the ability to differentiate between opposites, the faculty upon which human consciousness is based. In psychological terms, then, the idea of Paradise is linked to the pre-conscious stage of infancy in which the ego, as the center of human consciousness, has not yet been activated. As Neumann writes:

> With the emergence of the fully-fledged ego, the paradisal situation is abolished; the infantile condition, in which life was regulated by something ampler and more embracing, is at an end, and with it the natural dependence on that ample embrace. We may think of this paradisal situation in terms of religion, and say that everything was controlled by God; or we may formulate it ethically, and say that everything was still good and that evil had not yet come into the world. Other myths dwell on the "effortlessness" of the Golden Age, when nature was bountiful, and toil, suffering and pain did not exist; others stress the "everlastingness" of the Golden Age, the deathlessness of such an existence.[1]

Neumann seems to suggest here that the myth of Paradise graphically expresses a real, primal human experience, that of the infant. But surely no infant lives in a fantasy world containing such

[1]Neumann, *The Origins and History of Consciousness*, pp. 114–115.

25

sophisticated images of the Paradise myth. These are, rather, symbolic formulations of pre-conscious, pre-lingual experiences which have subsequently been given verbal and perceptual expression. The myth itself tells us that paradisial existence cannot be "known." With the knowledge of good and evil, of male and female, Paradise is forfeited. To "know" what Paradise means presupposes knowledge of its opposite, of the burdens and sufferings of earthly existence. The very idea of Paradise contains simultaneous grief over its loss.

The paradisal pre-ego time is also characterized as "existence in unitary reality," because in it there is not yet any polarization between inner and outer, subject and object, ego and Self. The state of total exteriorization, in which the child has not yet separated itself from the mother and from the world, may be regarded as existence in a total *participation mystique*, a universal extension of being, which constitutes the psychic amniotic fluid in which everything is still "suspended" and out of which the polarities of ego and Self, subject and object, person and world, have yet to crystalize . . . One can do justice to the psychic reality of this phase only by formulating it paradoxically. If you speak of objectless self-love[2] you must also speak of subjectless all-love, as

[2]Neumann is referring here to Freud's hypothesis of a primary narcissism "in which the infantile ego is sufficient unto itself." (Sigmund Freud, *The Complete Psychological Works*, Vol. 18, p. 110). This primary narcissism "continues until the ego begins to invest the image of objects with libido, transforming narcissistic libido into object libido" (ibid., Vol 23, p. 150). Primary Narcissism was seen as being subjectively identical to the "oceanic feeling" of universal extension. It was Michael Balint (*Primary Love and Psycho-Analytic Technique*, pp. 93-115) who, in 1937, first proposed an alternative concept, in the form of an initial "mother-child unity" or "primary object relation." Since then many studies have appeared on early pre-Oedipal development, particularly in the first year of life. Among writers on Analytical Psychology, Michael Fordham is outstanding in this regard. He sees Neumann's ideas on the infant's first year as containing excessive speculative generalizations. The important point, as far as Fordham is concerned, is that the infant begins in a state of initial unity, as a "primary self," and that the establishment of a relationship to the mother already involves considerable complexity and is not free from conflict. He points out that "Non-conflictual states can be experienced from time to time by children and adults, and it seems likely that infants experience more of them" ("The Self as an Imaginative Construct," *Journal of Analytical Psychology*, Vol. 24, 1979, p. 27). This in no way contradicts my own contention that the "longing for Paradise" relates to conflict-free states, even though it must be assumed that conflicts already crop up during infancy. If I understand him correctly, Neumann too is realistic enough to realize the virtual impossibility of a completely conflict-free primal relationship.

well as of a subjectless and objectless totally-being-loved. In the completely instinctual condition of pre-ego universal extension, in which the infant's world, mother and own body are undifferentiated, total connectedness is as characteristic as total narcissism.[3]

Thus the unitary reality embraces mother and infant, with the mother not yet perceived as a separate, independent entity. She is an integral component of primal infant experience, is simply "there," symbiotically woven into the infant's fabric of needs.

[3]Erich Neumann, "Narcissism, Normal Self-Formation and the Primary Relation to the Mother," in *Spring* 1966. New York: The Analytical Psychology Club of New York, p. 108.

3. The Socio-Psychological Relevance of the Primal Relationship

The illuminating research of biologist Adolf Portmann has shown that this early infantile phase is of decisive importance in matters of social psychology. Portmann has demonstrated that, compared to the young of other advanced mammals, the human child comes into the world at a low level of development. It needs an entire year before reaching the degree of maturity at which other mammals are born. Portmann therefore terms this first year of life "extra-uterine gestation." He writes:

> The outstanding characteristic of the higher mammals' development is the growth and maturation of the entire organization within the protection of the mother's body. All higher mammals are characterized by long periods of gestation, the duration of which is clearly related to the central nervous system's level of organization. Formed in the maternal uterus, and determined by the genetic plan specific to each species, is the entire apparatus of movement, the bodily posture appropriate to the species, and its typical instinctual organization, all of it tailored to an environment which is also genetically assigned to that species. Patterns of movement and behavior are formed in the mother's body, well-removed from later stimulus sources and yet oriented toward those subsequent stimuli, toward the future environment. Species-appropriate behavior begins immediately after birth, with regard to both motility and sense perception.[1]

[1]A. Portmann, *Zoologie und das neue Bild des Menschen* (Zoology and the New Image of Man). Hamburg: Rowohlt, 1958, p. 68.

For these reasons Portmann calls the higher mammals "fugitives from the nest," in contrast to such "nest squatters" as the birds, which develop fully and become capable of flight before leaving the nest. But in the case of humans, who are counted among the higher mammals, the situation is paradoxical, since the human child is in fact a typical "nest squatter" until the end of its first year.

Portmann points out that a newborn human has species-specific maturity neither in its type of movement nor its bodily posture nor its method of communication. Instead of maturing to that stage within the womb, as do the young of other higher mammals, the human infant is forced out into the world at a much earlier stage.[2] Hence Portmann labels the human being a "secondary nest squatter." It takes a year for a human child to develop the species-specific upright gait and to begin learning the species-specific form of communication, human speech. Portmann links this fact to the specifically human mode of existence, which is also built into Nature's plan. Compared to animal behavior, which the biologist terms "environment-linked and instinct-secured," specifically human behavior is characterized by "openness to the world and free will."

> It is our purpose [in using these terms] to emphasize the positive sides of a portentous, complex fact which has sometimes been evaluated differently. Often enough the negative aspects of the same phenomenon have been overemphasized, with humanity presented as instinctless, exiled from the security of the animal's environment-linked behavior. Sometimes, in such presentations, Man truly seems like a prisoner released from jail with inadequate means and put out on the streets of life.[3]

It is in keeping with mankind's "openness to the world" that our social fabric is not given to us genetically but must constitute itself anew in each individual through a mixture of hereditary factors on the one hand and, on the other, contact with external reality and the world around us.

> This unique aspect of human development is assured by the fact that human infants, though born in a quite advanced state in terms

[2]Ibid., p. 69.
[3]Ibid., p. 67.

of both form and psyche, [come into the world] long before the maturation of their species-specific forms of behavior. It is for the full development of those behavior patterns that the possibilities are given for contact with the environment, a rich experience of the world and social interchange.[4]

The period of "extra-uterine gestation" thus is of decisive importance to the human being as a conscious, social creature.

One of Portmann's former disciples, F. Renggli, questions Portmann's assumption that extra-uterine gestation is specific to the human species, pointing out that a similarly delayed process of motor maturation may be observed among the higher apes.[5] But aside from that qualification, he agrees with Portmann about the species-specific importance of the human child's prolonged dependence on its mother. He also adds a number of significant nuances. For example, he suggests that early forms of active contact-seeking (smiling, babbling) are specifically human, and that, all in all, the human child's extended period of dependency on the mother results in a much more intense experience of its own role in the mother-child relationship, laying the groundwork for ego-consciousness.

In any event, at a very early stage in its development the infant is exposed to "social" influences which have a powerfully formative effect on its subsequent development. The early unitary reality is at the same time the infant's first relation to something outside itself, to a "thou"—what Neumann has termed the primal relationship (*Urbeziehung*). This initial relation between mother and child is unique because it does not yet contain a polarity between "automorphous self-development and thou-relation."[6] It is for this reason that the mother in this phase is also termed a "narcissistic object." From the standpoint of the child she seems to exist only to serve its own gratification and not as a separate, independent being.

This is a pattern of relationship often to be found in adult life as well. In marriage and in close friendships, the partner, with his or her own autonomy and needs, is often perceived only as a

[4]Ibid., p. 77.
[5]F. Renggli, *Angst und Geborgenheit* (Fear and Security). Reinbek: Rowohlt, 1976, p. 78.
[6]Neumann, *The Child*, p. 14.

wholly-owned fulfiller of needs, a source of gratification. Such a drive for paradisial fulfillment, for total unity in a twosome, generally ends in disappointment. In the long run the expectations and needs of two partners can never be totally harmonized; a certain degree of conflict is inevitable. In a mature, adult relationship each partner's needs and expectations must remain flexible enough to be modified in the light of the other's psychic reality.

The primal relationship is so unique and paradisial because the mother-figure may, with what we might term legitimate ruthlessness, be experienced and used as the source of one's own well-being. At the same time, however, the human infant is totally at the mercy of the primary person in its environment, which can be a terribly dangerous situation that can transform Paradise into a Hell of suffering and deprivation. This will be dealt with in detail at a later point.

The paradisial "primal unity" is lost as the realization gradually dawns that the mother is a relatively independent "object." This is necessary in order for the child to begin experiencing itself as "subject" and "I."

4. Maturation and Development in Early Childhood

In the post-Freudian era many detailed studies have been published on the processes of infant maturation and development, with the mother included as part of the picture. But as yet there is no consensus about many points in this early phase. (One problem, of course, is that of near-total amnesia. It is commonly accepted that people cannot really remember the experiences of their first year.)

In some studies data are gathered from direct observation of the infant and its interaction with the mother (M. S. Mahler, J. Robertson, D. W. Winnicott, among others). In other instances very early experiences are "reconstructed" in the course of analysis of older children and adults, since it is assumed on the basis of empirical evidence that many phenomena observable in an analysand's transference to the analyst are facsimiles of very early experiences and therefore permit certain hypothetical conclusions to be drawn about the individual's earliest history.

C. G. Jung did not publish any systematic, detailed studies on the earliest processes of development and maturation, although certain essays contained in Volume 17 of the Collected Works (*The Development of Personality*) provide important insights into the psychology of the child. Erich Neumann has dealt extensively with this subject, however. Under the leadership of Michael Fordham,[1] the British school of Analytical Psychology has also

[1]Michael Fordham, "Individuation and Ego Development," in *Journal of Analytical Psychology*, Vol. III, No. 2 (1958), London; *Children as Individuals*,

published extensive findings in this area, developing a fruitful synthesis with the views of such psychoanalytic thinkers as M. Klein and D. W. Winnicott. A detailed examination of Fordham's interesting observations on the process of individuation in the development of the child's ego, however, would exceed the bounds of the present study.

In a brief and somewhat oversimplified form, the following might be said from the standpoint of Analytical Psychology:

A child is born into the world equipped with certain predispositions which make possible survival and species-appropriate maturation. These predispositions are expressed in the infant's instinctual needs, the satisfaction of which is dependent upon an external "object." In this context C. G. Jung states:

> The form of the world into which [man] is born is already inborn in him as a virtual image. Likewise parents, wife, children, birth and death are inborn in him as virtual images, as psychic aptitudes. These *a priori* categories have by nature a collective character; they are images of parents, wife and children in general, and are not individual predestinations. We must therefore think of these images as lacking in solid content, hence as unconscious. They only acquire solidity, influence, and eventual consciousness in the encounter with empirical facts, which touch the unconscious aptitude and quicken it to life.[2]

There is an inborn, archetypal aptitude or readiness to actualize the image of the Maternal in the early phase of life. It might be said that the infant brings with it into the world a predisposition to experience "Mother and mothering." We know that the image of the mother must undergo a process of maturation, since, as we have seen, the newborn infant cannot perceive its mother in her independent totality as an "object." Therefore, according to Melanie Klein,[3] it is the "part objects" of the mother or of its own body which first become significant to the infant. Above all it is the maternal breast which appears to stimulate the first fantasies,

---

London: Hodder & Stroughton, 1969; "Maturation of Ego and Self in Infancy," in *Analytical Psychology—A Modern Science* (Library of Analytical Psychology, Vol. 1). London: 1973; *Self and Autism* (Library of Analytical Psychology, Vol. 3). London: 1976; "The Self as an Imaginative Construct," *Journal of Analytical Psychology*, Vol. 24, 1979.

[2] C. G. Jung, *Collected Works*, Vol. 7, New York: Pantheon Books, for the Bollingen Foundation, p. 190.

[3] *The Psychoanalysis of Children*. New York: Dell, 1976.

being imaged either as good and nourishing or as punitive and withholding. At the same time, as a part of the mother, the breast also represents the entire mother.

In contrast to Klein's view, Neumann emphasizes that in the early phase of the *Urbeziehung* the mother is experienced as the containing and nourishing "world." But it does not seem to me that this approach necessarily contradicts the "part object" theory. Part objects may be regarded as fixed points around which the first fantasy contents are grouped, but as such they are certainly components of the mother as "world."

Winnicott[4] postulates that the mother has a double function for the infant, in whose experience she is both "object mother" and "environment mother." As "environment mother" she attends to the infant's environment, protecting, caring for and carrying the child, giving it a sense of security, while as "object mother" she is the possessor of certain "part objects" which can fulfill its most pressing needs. Winnicott also observes that the infant needs the illusion that it can itself create the mother or the breast. The "objective" reality of breast and mother slowly becomes an internalized experience of the child. But a certain amount of time and latitude is required for the infant to somewhat harmonize its archetypal expectations with the real object, by playing and experimenting with it. In this way it forms the image of a convincingly real breast and mother as a source of gratification, and also as a target of greedy attack and biting.

The infantile relation to part objects may also play a part in adult functioning. For example, someone may describe a personal characteristic of his/her mother and believe that in doing so he has captured her entire nature or personality. He may see his mother as only negative, ugly, primitive, strong, or as only good and beautiful. Such a description is based on projections through which, out of our own archetypal needs, we "create" (or at least shape and reshape) people in the world around us.[5] In reality, however, even the best of mothers cannot gratify all her child's needs perfectly and immediately, cannot always prevent or in-

[4]*The Maturational Processes and the Facilitating Environment*. New York: International University Press, 1965.
[5]S. K. Lambert, "Archetypische Funktionen, Objektbeziehungen und internalisierte Objekte" (Archetypal Functions, Object Relations and Internalized Objects), in *Zeitschrift fur analytische Psychologie*, Vol. 8, No. 1, 1977.

stantly soothe unpleasant bodily sensations and early anxieties. There are frustrations—to use a well-worn term—which arise from the juxtaposition of paradisial expectations and human limitations.

As the child gradually learns to perceive its mother as a whole person it simultaneously experiences her limitations and her separation from itself. In this way it also learns that it, too, is limited, confined to its own body and separated from the mother. This is the first intimation of the human condition described by the philosopher Heidegger as "being thrown back upon oneself." This sense of self-being and self-becoming, however, is also powerfully attractive and normally serves to liberate developmental energies. The fluctuation between symbiotic needs on the one hand, and the need for independence and individuation on the other, has been carefully described and extensively treated by M. S. Mahler.[6]

According to Neumann, the successive appearance of the mother archetype in more human form is typical of the later phase of the primal relationship. He writes:

> Here again, to be sure, the mother is an archetype, not only a personal, individual mother; that is, she is the *Great* Mother and Mother Goddess; but at the same time she has become a human mother. The functions that were previously performed by the anonymous, formless world in which the still undelineated child "floated"—the functions of containing, nourishing, warming and protecting—are now humanized. That is, they are experienced in the person of the mother who, at first in isolated moments, then continuously, is experienced and known as an individual human being.[7]

From the standpoint of Analytical Psychology, then, the entire early phase of unitary reality and the primal relationship occurs under the dominance of the mother archetype. It should be evident by now that we are dealing here with the experience of "the Maternal" itself, the archetypal disposition and need to experience those things which are generally ascribed to the realm of the Maternal. The child experiences the Maternal long before it grows aware of the individuality of its own personal mother.

[6]*On Human Symbiosis and the Vicissitudes of Individuation*. New York: International University Press, 1968.
[7]Neumann, *The Child*, p. 24.

5. The Phenomenology of the Mother Archetype

Some general explanatory remarks on the mother archetype would seem appropriate at this point. In Analytical Psychology this term is used to denote the predisposition to a broad range of human experience and behavior. It is difficult to describe, define and clearly circumscribe the significance of the mother archetype in discursive language. What is meant might be described as the experience of connectedness, relatedness to, and even dependence upon, what we term Nature in the broadest sense.

We commonly speak of Mother Nature and Mother Earth. Both in the external world and in the inner landscape of the psyche, Nature presents itself to us as our own instinctual nature. C. G. Jung often spoke of Eros in connection with the mother archetype, as opposed to the Logos quality of the father archetype.[1] Eros, in this context, means relatedness to the state of natural being within us and around us; drives, impulses, feelings, intimations, are its psychic functions. The word "matter" is also derived from the Latin word for mother (*mater*). Hence this archetype represents psychic elements related to the experience of the material, the concrete, the physical body and its needs.

The symbolism of such modes of experience—that is, the range of images that represent existence in, or relation to, the maternal

[1]The importance of the father archetype will be examined in Chapter 10.

36

realm—is of virtually endless variety.[2] Jung enumerates the following as among the more characteristic:

> . . . the personal mother and grandmother, stepmother and mother-in-law; then any woman with whom a relationship exists —for example, a nurse or governess or perhaps a remote ancestress. Then there are what might be termed mothers in a figurative sense. To this category belongs the goddess, and especially the Mother of God, the Virgin and Sophia . . . things representing the goal of our longing for redemption, such as Paradise, the Kingdom of God, the Heavenly Jerusalem. Many things arousing devotion or feelings of awe, as for instance the Church, university, city or country, heaven, earth, the woods, the sea or any still waters, matter even, the underworld and the moon, can be mother-symbols . . . . things and places standing for fertility and fruitfulness: the cornucopia, a ploughed field, a garden . . . a rock, a cave, a tree, a spring, a deep well . . . various vessels such as the baptismal font . . . vessel-shaped flowers like the rose or the lotus . . . and of course, the uterus, *yoni*, and anything of a like shape. Added to this list there are many animals, such as the cow, hare, and helpful animals in general.[3]

Within this symbolism the emphasis is sometimes stronger on the containing-sheltering "environment mother" (Paradise, the Church, university, city, garden, cave, oven, vessel, etc.) and sometimes on the "object mother" (human forms of the maternal, also the milk-giving cow or the spring of water as the thirst-quenching source of gratification). In this context, the symbolism of birth and transformation is also of great significance (uterus, vagina, a deep well, a spring as source, the baptismal font, an oven as the potential for transformation and rebirth). Neumann writes of two distinct aspects of the Great Feminine: the elementary and the transformative.[4]

In the context of this study, we find an important symbolic representation of the primal relationship in the many images depicting a divine mother holding (and often nursing) her divine

[2]See Neumann, *The Great Mother*, and Jung, *Collected Works*, Vol. 9, I, "Psychological Aspects of the Mother Archetype."
[3]*Collected Works*, Vol. 9, I, p. 81.
[4]*The Great Mother.*

child. Statuettes of this kind, some of them dating from prehistoric times, have been found at many sites. One of the most beautiful examples comes from Egypt at about 2000 B.C.; it shows the goddess Isis with her infant son Horus, and such is its artistic quality that the contact of skin, breast and eyes between mother and child is impressively evident (Figure 4).

In Western culture the main analogy would be the countless representations of the Madonna and Child. Many of these strikingly show the unity of two mutually related creatures. In doing so, they more or less present an image of the Mother of All Mothers and the Infant of All Infants—a pattern, an eternal model, as it were. And since the image is perceived as eternal, the association with an immortal goddess is quite understandable. Every infant—whether born to a Bushman mother or a modern career woman—needs the experience of the primal relationship and the unitary reality for its existence and the development of its human potential.

The mother archetype thus primarily evokes experiences of internal and external "Nature" by means of basic drives, impulses, feelings and intimations. But we cannot content ourselves with an idealized description confined to the life-giving, sheltering and gratifying aspects of the maternal. Mother Nature creates life, but "she" also brings death. She is creative *and* destructive, protecting (e.g., by means of the survival instinct) *and* cruel (most species of animals live at the expense of others). Natural calamity, pernicious illness and destructive fury are also parts of her realm.

Seen as "the rule of Nature," the mother archetype is ambivalent, ethically neutral, neither good nor evil. Jung writes that the symbols of the mother archetype may have "a positive, favorable meaning or a negative, evil meaning."[5] Many symbols emphasize the negative aspects of the mother archetype, for example, images that involve being devoured, typified by the dragon, the whale, the devouring witch (as in "Hansel and Gretel"). In addition to positive images of the primal relationship showing the unity of mother and child, there are such powerful negative images as the child-eating goddess Kali in India or Rangda in Bali.[6] The grave,

[5]*Collected Works*, Vol. 9, I, pp. 81–82.
[6]See Neumann, *The Great Mother*, Figs. 66 and 71.

4. *Isis with Horus.*
   Copper, Egypt about 2000 B.C.
   The Egyptian Wing, Berlin State Museum.

sarcophagus and Hell itself are symbols of the "environment mother" in her torturing, death-dealing aspect.

The "negative transformative character"[7] of the mother archetype is expressed in figures that have the power to enchant people or turn them to stone: Circe transforms men into swine, the Gorgon Medusa, with her serpentine hair, petrifies them, and witches in fairytales and folklore can turn people into animals. Then there is the castrating mother goddess, typified by Cybele of Asia Minor, whose priests had to sacrifice their virility. The negative form of the Great Mother, then, can bring life to a halt, evoke emotional emptiness, petrifaction, blockage of the creative imagination and of orgasmic potency. She can also transform a person into an animal—i.e., cause an uncontrollable outbreak of animal drives.

The foregoing is a mere sketch of the many modes of the mother archetype. All of them are inherent as dispositions. But which of these dispositions will be constellated in a given individual at a particular time will depend largely on the phase of development of his/her consciousness, the attitude toward psychic contents, and the reactions of the environment toward archetypal needs.

Even though an infant cannot yet imagine the complex symbolism of the mother archetype, its primal experience is played out within that arena. The maternal breast—whether perceived as good and nourishing, evil and attacking, or merely withholding —is an experience the nature of which depends primarily upon the behavior of the personal mother. It is of paramount importance that the ground be laid during the period of the primal relationship for a predominance of positive maternal images. The infant can then give itself to the positive maternal with calm confidence, laying the groundwork for the "basic trust"[8] which is the source of self-confidence and solidly grounded relationships with others.

Obviously the mother archetype not only has its effect upon the child, but also influences the experiences and perceptions of the personal mother. A woman who goes through pregnancy and

---

[7] *The Great Mother.*
[8] Erik H. Erikson, *Childhood and Society.* New York: W. W. Norton & Co., 1950.

then cares for her newborn child brings to all of this her own individuality, her specific marriage experiences, perhaps a professional background. What happens to her during pregnancy and after the birth of her child? She is no longer the same, her life has changed. She has become a mother. That is to say, something inside her has awakened to life. Things happen within her over which she has no control. She cannot control whether the fruit of her womb will ripen properly, or when it will be born, or if she will be able to nurse it. All of this takes place within her "naturally." Mother Nature is doing her work via hormonal changes, among other things. The woman feels the process of becoming a mother in her own body, part of which is the activation of many related images. She must react somehow to the experience of the maternal within her. And her attitude toward the activating mother archetype will at the same time influence her attitude toward the child.

Just how this species-appropriate maternity will manifest itself in a particular woman, and how she will react to it, depends on her individual situation and her particular compound of personal factors. At the same time the *Zeitgeist*, the spirit of the times, and the social norms emanating from it, also play their part. The attitudes and customs of a woman's social class exert considerable influence on each mother's behavior patterns.

Of decisive importance in this context is how the mother-image operates within the psyche of each individual woman, whether it is predominantly the nourishing-sheltering aspect or the devouring aspect that is felt even at the unconscious level—in other words, whether the woman's own experiences in infancy served to instill basic trust or gave rise to a predominance of basic mistrust. If the tone is set by the negative-devouring aspect of the mother archetype, with its attendant basic mistrust, what happens in concrete terms may be something like this:

The mother finds that every spontaneous interaction with her child is clouded by doubt and mistrust. She experiences constant anxiety that she is somehow "not doing right by" the child, which makes the mother-child relationship a great emotional burden that "devours" all joy. As a result the mother feels herself overtaxed and can barely suppress her resentment of her burdensome offspring. This in turn generates guilt feelings, in which she berates herself for being incapable of loving her child properly or of being a decent mother to it. Such guilt feelings often mask unconscious desires to be free of the child. These horrid intimations, prompted by the inner "death mother," are generally overcompensated by outbreaks of inappropriate and exaggerated attention and anxiety.

The entire complex prevents a relaxed and empathic dealing with the child's needs. The existence of the infant is not experienced as gratifying and therefore no joy radiates outward to the child. The ground is thus laid for the child to perceive itself as superfluous in the world, rather than accepted and supported. In this way neurosis is often passed on from generation to generation. The practice of every psychotherapist includes many adult emotional disturbances which can be traced back to such distortions in the primal relationship. So it would be worthwhile at this point to briefly examine this phenomenon, which can have negative consequences in every social context.

6. Disturbances of the Primal Relationship as an Infantile Hell

As Neumann writes, "Because the early, uroboric phase of child development is characterized by a minimum of discomfort and tension, and a maximum of well-being and security, as well as by the unity of I and thou, Self and world, it is known to myth as paradisiacal." Neumann also speaks of the "uroboric state of containment 'in the Round.'"[1]

But the Paradise of early infancy is dependent upon the maternal care tendered by the person in charge of the child. There is always the danger that the balance may shift to a minimum of well-being and security and a maximum of discomfort and tension, turning the infant's experience of Paradise into that of Hell. This occurs when the person playing the maternal role is not "good enough" (to use D. W. Winnicott's phrase) at fulfilling the vital infantile needs for attention and security.

Such disturbances are not always caused by a mother who consciously or unconsciously rejects her maternal function and is therefore unable to provide enough emotional attention. Early physical complaints or sickness in the infant may result in premature disruption of its existence in the paradisial unitary reality, later giving rise to the same psychic disturbances as those evoked through emotional rejection by the mother. The infant cannot yet differentiate as to whether the source of its painful discomfort is outside or inside its own body. But it is beyond

[1] *The Child*, pp. 14, 15.

43

question that, even if feeding and bodily care are perfectly adequate, shortcomings in emotional attention during the first year of life can result in very severe disturbances in the child.

It was R. A. Spitz who first called attention to this fact, which he discovered as a result of his research into the lives of institutionalized children.[2] Emotionally deprived children develop very early depressions, for which Spitz coined the term "hospitalism." The symptoms are vomiting, disturbances of digestion and sleep, general passivity, etc. To illustrate this phenomenon I cite some comments recorded by Spitz concerning his observations in a foundling home:

> We observed total deprivation and its consequences in a Foundling Home situated outside of the United States, housing 91 infants . . . In this institution the children were breast-fed during their first three months by their own mothers, or by one of the other mothers, if the child's own mother was not available. During these three months the infants had the appearance (and tested out at the developmental level) of average normal children of the same city.
>
> After the third month mother and child were separated. The infants remained in the Foundling Home, where they were adequately cared for in every bodily respect. Food, hygiene, medical care and medication, etc., were as good as, or even superior to, that of any other institutions we have observed.
>
> But, as one single nurse had to care for eight children (officially: actually up to twelve children would devolve to the care of one nurse), they were emotionally starved. To put it drastically, they got approximately one-tenth of the normal affective supplies provided in the usual mother-child relationship.
>
> After separation from their mothers, these children went through the stages of progressive deterioration characteristic for partial deprivation . . . Soon, after the relatively brief period of three months, a new clinical picture appeared: motor retardation became fully evident; the children became completely passive; they lay supine in their cots. They did not achieve the motor control necessary to turn into the prone position. The face became vacuous, eye coordination defective, the expression often imbecile . . .

[2]René A. Spitz, *The First Year of Life*. New York: International Universities Press, 1965.

In our tests these children showed a progressive decline of the developmental quotient. By the end of the second year, the average of their developmental quotients stands at 45 per cent of the normal. This would be the level of the idiot. We continued to observe these children at longer intervals up to the age of four years . . . By that time, with a few exceptions, these children cannot sit, stand, walk or talk.[3]

Spitz adds that, despite excellent physical care, the mortality rate among such children is very high.

This devastating picture clearly shows how right Portmann is in emphasizing the newborn child's dependence on "early contact with the richness of the world," that is, on attention and stimulation by the maternal environment. In a successful primal relationship the mother-figure compensates for unpleasant and threatening factors: hunger, excessive cold or warmth, lying in wet diapers, the discomfort of colds, painful ailments, anxieties. It has also been discovered that eye contact, body contact, the mother's voice, even perception of the maternal heartbeat, are of great importance for the infant's development.

The early phase of infancy should, moreover, be kept as free as possible from deprivation. Meyerhofer[4] makes a strong plea for nursing a child whenever it shows signs of hunger, rather than according to a rigid timetable. She cites her own frequent observation of cases in which infants have demonstrated eating problems after only ten days of post-natal hospital care with regularly scheduled feedings. In such cases she generally advises the mother to adjust herself to the child's rhythm in feeding, a procedure for which she claims unvarying success. Mechanical clock time is not necessarily in harmony with an infant's "instinctive time." Feeding by the clock introduces an alien, rational element into the infant's world; it is a premature training measure designed to make the child conform to our competitive society, for which the hands of the clock are an eloquent symbol.

A mother's adjustment to her infant's instinctual needs presupposes a certain degree of empathy. Under favorable conditions a process takes place by which a mother is sensitized to the needs

[3]Ibid., pp. 278–279.
[4]M. Meyerhofer, from an unpublished lecture, Zurich, c. 1967.

of her child. At the same time, of course, a mother's own gratification, her joy in the dialogue with her baby, plays an important
part in the crucial harmony of the early relationship. No mother
should be expected (or expect herself) to make superhuman
sacrifices for her child; she, too, is human, with her own conflicts
and mood swings. A natural acceptance of one's limitations is certainly more beneficial to the basic harmony in the primal relationship than a cramped, rigid exercise in duty and self-sacrifice. It
is for this reason that Winnicott rightly speaks not of "perfect
motherliness" but rather of maternal caring that is "good
enough." In any event, a predominance of the "good" over the
"terrible" mother is vitally important for a child's development.

This development naturally includes the unfolding of a species-
appropriate consciousness. The center of human consciousness
—referred to by Jung as the ego, or ego-complex—is grounded,
formed and developed in the primal relationship. Neumann
speaks of the formation of

> a positive-integral ego capable of integrating positive and negative
> factors in such a way that the unity of the personality is guaranteed
> and is not split into antagonistic parts . . . . Thus—to use an ab-
> breviated formulation—there arises a positive tolerance on the part
> of the ego which, on the basis of its attitude of security and con-
> fidence toward the mother, is capable of accepting the world and
> itself, because it has a constant experience of positive tolerance
> and acceptedness through the mother.[5]

Disturbances of the primal relationship are characterized in
greater or lesser degree by a predominance of the archetypal
"terrible mother" image. In such cases ego development is not
grounded in "the fertile soil of the motherland." R. A. Spitz has
described the extreme forms of such negative development. Having experienced a disturbed primal relationship in infancy, adults
may go through life with a basic sense that there is absolutely
nothing to rely on, neither out in the world nor inside themselves.
They are plagued, in other words, by a more or less powerful,
free-floating anxiety. The result is rejection of their own inner
vitality and mistrustful isolation from their environment. The expectation of being rejected by the people around them leads to

5*The Child*, pp. 58–59.

constant difficulty with relationships. Other people are seldom seen as they are, but rather misapprehended as parts of a rejecting or devouring "environment mother." Such individuals are generally oversensitive to every nuance in the behavior of others, prone to interpret the slightest dissonance as rejection or offense. This hypersensitivity and querulousness in turn provoke rejection from others.

In most such people the trait of aggressiveness, itself a necessary function of the life instinct, has not been sufficiently integrated into the personality and brought under conscious control. As Neumann puts it: "The pathological situation of a child abandoned in its helplessness and dependency causes it to erupt into rage and aggression, or in terms of the symbolism of the alimentary stage, into a cannibalistic, sadistic desire to devour its mother."[6] In later life uncontrolled aggression, liable to break out at the slightest provocation, and intense envy of all those who "have it so good" are generally symptomatic of a disturbed primal relationship.

Quite often, however, uncontrolled aggression is even more strongly directed inward, in the form of masochistic self-accusations and severe guilt feelings. Neumann continues, "The Great Mother Figure of the primal relationship is a goddess of fate who, by her favor or disfavor, decides over life and death, positive or negative development; and moreover, her attitude is the supreme judgment, so that her defection is identical with a nameless guilt on the part of the child."[7] In addition to generalized anxiety, an intense, irrational sense of guilt is indeed symptomatic of a disturbed primal relationship. There is no lack of "proof" to confirm the sense of one's own wrongness, since the aggressive impulses of anger and envy stemming from the problematical primal relationship are often intensely active, keeping the vicious cycle in motion: "If I'm so bad, I deserve to be punished and rejected—even by my therapist."

To illustrate all of this I shall briefly cite two cases from my own practice. The first involves a 22-year-old girl with a severe neurosis, the symptoms of which were typical of a disturbed primal relationship. This analysand felt herself to be the stupidest

[6]Ibid., p. 76.
[7]Ibid., p. 87.

and ugliest of people, rejected and ridiculed by the whole world. Every spark of internal vitality, every desire, wish or thought of her own, was accompanied by intense guilt feelings.

In reality this young woman was neither ugly nor stupid. She was actually very talented and quite original. But she could not hold on to a job, because soon after taking up each new position she would feel herself unwanted. Her behavior inevitably provoked rejection, so that time and again she was fired for being "uncooperative." Frequently she would not show up for work because she feared that she would be dismissed.

The same scenario was played out in her analysis, in her transference-relationship with me. On the one hand she was desperate to be accepted and loved by me, and there was a genuine inclination to help in working through her problems. But at the same time she felt compelled to provoke my rejection and constantly accused me of hating and scorning her.

The case history revealed that her mother had been physically and mentally ill during her pregnancy and at the time of my patient's birth. The child seemed to her an unbearable burden. When I began treating this young woman, her mother had been dead for five years.

One day, early in the analysis, she wrote down some memories of her mother. This marked the first time that she had dared to venture a few cautiously critical remarks about her mother's behavior—with the result that she was terribly frightened the very next night by the following dream: Her mother appeared to her as a powerful spirit and read everything she had written in her journal. Upon awakening, plagued by guilt, she determined never again to say or write anything "bad" about her mother. There followed countless dreams in which her mother, appearing in various forms as a powerful or superhuman creature, opposed and stamped out her repeated attempts at self-liberation.

During our therapy sessions every negative statement about her mother was accompanied by enormous guilt feelings. I therefore suggested that we call this powerful, negative mother-figure within her "Kali" (an Indian mother goddess, depicted primarily as devouring and death-dealing).[8] In so doing I told her that

8Neumann, *The Great Mother*.

there was no need for us to make any accusations against her own mother, that it had not been entirely her fault and that in her way she had tried to do her best. But her mother had also been forced by Kali to act in an anti-life manner and thus to evoke a negative sense of the world in her child. I explained that the hatred this young woman felt toward her mother, which caused her such intense guilt, was thus not really directed against her personal mother but against this witch Kali, with whom we would have to deal together. In this way I succeeded in reducing her guilt feelings. (It is indeed fruitless to direct hatred against one's own mother when her emotional abuse of her child has been done in innocence, out of her own psychological illness.)

For nearly two years this analysand subjected our relationship to every possible test and stress. She repeatedly accused me of pretending to be on her side only out of professional duty. She insisted that she perceived quite clearly how much I despised her. She would stop coming, stop being a burden to me, etc. In other words, her ego-consciousness repeatedly fell victim to the negative mother archetype, which did not want to let her live and develop. To dare trusting in human relationships is to live; to close oneself off means inner emptiness and death.

After almost two years she had come far enough to feel genuine confidence in our relationship. This helped constellate the other side of the mother archetype, the fundamental sense of security, nourishment and natural growth. Dreams now appeared with blossoming, springlike landscapes, ideal settings for the experience of maternal caring and attention. Supported by the security of our relationship, she finally dared to examine and comprehend the causal relationships in her own life more objectively and without great feelings of guilt. Her self-confidence grew and she found employment appropriate to her real nature, a position which gave her pleasure and in which she was appreciated accordingly. She learned to see the world around her more realistically and not to be so threatened by her projective fantasies of inevitable rejection.

Another analysand, a young woman of 25, had a dream which portrayed a disturbed primal relationship and at the same time expressed a hope for redemption: "It takes place in the Middle Ages. I am in an alpine valley with another girl. Everything is governed by bewitched cows, and we ourselves are bewitched. Suddenly I am grabbed by one of the enchanted cows and dragged off into the darkness, through dark valleys. Somehow I know that letting myself be dragged along by the beast is the only path to salvation. The cow drags me into a village, where there is an outdoor stage. I am dragged onto this stage, and there the cow turns into a nice, very fatherly man. I am to dance with him. He shows me various dance steps, and I think: 'I can't do that.' I hear music and I try a dance step. Then I know that I will be saved as soon as this piece of music is over.''

The mother of this analysand was dedicated to a medieval-seeming Catholicism which provided the theme and justification of her depression: The world is a vale of tears; man as creature of instinct fell prey to Original Sin, and only remorse, atonement and constant prayer can lead to God's benevolence. It was in this emotional climate that my patient had been raised by her mother. This explains why the dream took place in the Middle Ages, and why instinctive, milk-giving and warmth-giving motherliness (symbolized by the cows) was perceived by the dreamer as bewitched. No trust could be placed in things pleasant or satisfying, or in one's own instinctive impulses; all of that was dangerous, sinful.

This young woman's basic problem was that she could not accept herself; she denied her own nature, felt ashamed at every statement she made and perceived herself as guilty and inferior. The other girl who was with her in the valley of the bewitched cows reminded her of a schoolmate who had been rejected by everyone. Her mother had tied her possessively to herself and had even managed to undermine her perfectly normal attachment to her father. At the start of the analysis, this young woman was still completely dependent on her know-it-all mother, who managed her finances and went with her to buy all her clothes. The daughter did not believe she was capable of choosing a dress by herself and was also afraid that the saleswomen would talk her into unwise purchases.

In the dream the masculine-paternal element appeared at first as one of the bewitched cows, but then took its own form. It underwent this transformation because the dreamer, despite her fear, was able to accept being dragged through the darkness as an ultimately redeeming experience. Here, of course, the analysis itself played its part. The fatherly man who appeared in place of the cow reminded the patient of me, her therapist. In this case the transference within the analysis was of vital therapeutic importance. Being dragged along, in the dream, meant giving herself up trustingly to an overwhelming experience.

In the analysis she was full of ambivalence and fear at first, expecting me to "gore" her, to "pin her to the wall," to ridicule and berate her, as her mother had always done. At the same time, in her fantasy I was the wise, understanding great father on whom she wished to rely. But such impulses were perceived as bad, damnable, dangerous. Her mother, after all, had succeeded in subverting her affections for her father (which is why the dream image representing the masculine-paternal was also bewitched at first). If, during our therapy sessions, the slightest impulse of feeling toward me came out, she would have to punish herself afterward. The punishment consisted of forbidding herself to think about me at all, which made her feel terribly isolated and often served to split off and castrate the effectiveness of our work. Moreover she feared that, although I was able to understand and accept much of what she said, deep down I thought of her as laughable and twisted. After each session she would think about the "stupid things" she had said and expected that at our next session I would berate or despise her for them, as her mother had so often done.

In short, it was extremely difficult for this young woman to feel and accept what sympathy came her way (as expressed in the dream image of dance and music). In her dream the spell was broken by a surrender to, and acceptance of, her own problems without having her sense of self-worth totally destroyed. The most difficult thing for this analysand was learning to accept herself as a total being, with light and dark sides. It was this sense of herself that had been repeatedly attacked by the witch-mother, and each time she had felt herself depressively bereft of the right to live.

The marked improvement experienced by both the analysands described here was possible because they came to perceive their therapist not just as a rejecting mother but ultimately as a more or less trusted, confidence-inspiring, accepting figure. The archetypal disposition to constellate the supportive, inner mother-image, nearly buried by their negative experiences, was regenerated (which is often not possible). As Neumann writes: "It would seem that virtually the only way in which this primary guilt feeling and its consequences can be reduced and resolved in the first half of life is through a situation of transference that reconstitutes the primal relationship and regenerates the damaged ego-Self axis."[9]

If it proves possible to reconstitute the primal relationship within the transference, the analysand feels a most intense need to remain part of the analyst forever, never to part from him/her, to be thus constantly contained and supported. The paradisial joy that is longed for in such a case is a kind of merging with the analyst. This places the therapist in a very difficult position which may endanger the success of the therapy. It is impossible for the analyst to concretely and completely fulfill the analysand's desire for the symbiotic Paradise of the primal relationship. The therapist may therefore again be perceived as a withholding or rejecting figure, thus restoring the old constellation of the disturbed primal relationship. Often such an outcome is unconsciously provoked by the analysand.

In this situation it is important that the analyst, whether male or female, bring empathy and understanding to bear and try to include consideration of the problem of denial in the "good enough" mothering which he or she is providing. Feelings of unrequited love in the analysand generate frustrated fury, pain, a sense of being victimized, mortified and humiliated. Even when they are directed against the analyst, the open expression of these emotions should be encouraged within the framework of the therapy as much as possible. They are, after all, largely an expression of the fury felt at the original mother.

It is vitally important that the analysand's rage over his "rejection" be allowed, and that it not shatter the analyst or his caring. The therapist must be able to withstand and accept the aggression directed against him, and must continue to be there for the patient in a role like that of the sheltering "environment mother." Of course, it is also important that the analysand learn to understand and accept all of this, with the aid of explanation and interpretation. In this process one must rely on those aspects of

[9]Neumann, *The Child*, p. 88.

psychic energy within the analysand which strive for independence, ego development and individuation, pushing to grow beyond the necessary but regressive symbiosis of the transference.

Finally, it should be stressed that the mere fact of a damaged primal relationship in infancy does not in itself constitute a prognosis. According to Neumann, "It is also necessary to consider the extent of the damage, the time of its inception, its duration, the way in which it has been compensated by the environment . . . the constitutional factors"[10]—all of which will combine to determine the degree of psychic disturbance and the specific symptoms in the adult.

On the other hand, the occurrence of the adult symptoms we have described does permit the conclusion that there was a more or less seriously disturbed primal relationship. Such an *Urbeziehung* lays the foundation for many future psychic disruptions and traumatic experiences, giving rise not to an integral ego but to a damaged ego incapable of dealing adequately with life's manifold problems.

[10]Ibid., p. 80.

7. Infant Paradise and Infant Hell: Links Between Primal Relationship and Cultural Canon Among Archaic Peoples

In the 1930s the British writer Aldous Huxley published a utopian novel dealing with the problem of "being happy." His now famous book *Brave New World* offers an imaginative depiction of an earthly Paradise in which all people can enjoy carefree, unconflicted, happy lives. But something had to happen before such a social order could be established: the elimination of the family, and particularly of the mother. There could be no more motherhood, neither in its individual, personal form nor in the archetypal sense of Mother Nature.

The world Huxley presents to us it based on deliberate manipulation. It is one in which biology and related technologies are so advanced that children can be bred exogenetically, that is, by synthetic means outside the body of a human mother. This makes possible their standardization even before they are "decanted" (no one in that world is born), so that they see the light of day genetically prepared for their predetermined caste and social and economic functions.

The more highly differentiated adjustment to each caste's desired social, work and consumer behavior is handled by a system of neo-Pavlovian conditioning based on hypnopaedia, or sleep-teaching. In the conditioning halls assigned to each caste, whispering loudspeakers inculcate sleeping youngsters with such gems of moral education as "Everyone belongs to everyone else." The secret of happiness and virtue, as one official puts it, is "liking what you've got to do. All conditioning aims at that: making people like their inescapable social destiny."

Sex in the brave new world is uninhibited from earliest childhood. Youngsters barely past the toddler stage are encouraged to engage in sexual play with members of the opposite sex. The only taboo is a continuation of sex with the same partner for a protracted period, since that raises the danger of intimate relationship. And in the event that inner conflicts should arise despite everything, there is plenty of distraction available: "feelies," scent organs, and if need be even soma, the perfect drug, which gives a person "a holiday from reality" and combines "all the advantages of Christianity and alcohol and none of their defects." Through sleep-teaching the people are conditioned from childhood to reach for this drug at the slightest provocation, as expressed in the hypnopaedic proverb: "One cubic centimetre cures ten gloomy sentiments."

So no one need suffer, and everyone's welfare is provided for in accordance with his or her genetically predetermined and conditioning-reinforced destiny. But all of this is possible thanks only to total denaturing and elimination of the concept of mother —one of the very few things to be regarded as obscene in this promiscuous society.

The absence of inner and outer conflict as portrayed here demands a complete leveling of emotional experience and can be achieved only by eliminating the mother as the source of earliest emotions. Huxley perceived this with psychological accuracy. Another aspect of such a society is that nothing must be permitted to take its natural course. Everything must be calculated, planned and controlled; with the aid of the most refined techniques, all social structures must be arranged to insure stability, as opposed to the living flux of nature. The archetype of the mother is thus artificially sterilized. It becomes a flat image of the environment mother who keeps her human children from maturing, provides for all their material needs and soothes their hurt with soma. Emotional ties—whether originating in love, hate or ambivalence— are to be avoided as sources of undesirable conflict.

The primal relationship is indeed relevant to social concerns. Aside from her individual personality, the manner in which a mother forms her relationship with her infant is strongly molded by social norms. And the social norms relating to child rearing in turn often amazingly reflect the values and goals of a particular society.

Many ethnological studies have supported the hypothesis of a link between forms of early mother-child relationship and a society's dominant cultural canon. Erik Erikson[1] reports his observations of two American Indian tribes he studied in this context: the Sioux, who were prairie hunters, and the Yurok, who live mainly by fishing the salmon-rich waters of the Klamath River. As former buffalo hunters, the Sioux saw to it that their child-training practices reinforced such valued characteristics as a ready hunting and fighting spirit, the inclination to do sadistic harm to the enemy, and the ability to stand extreme hardship and pain. Generosity was seen as an ethical ideal, since the sharing of the fortunate or skillful hunter's catch was of vital importance to the entire tribe.

The Sioux infant was lovingly nursed by its mother day or night, whenever it whimpered, and was also allowed to play freely with the breast. A small child was not allowed to cry in helpless frustration, but was immediately comforted and satisfied. The Sioux used to think that "whites want to estrange their children from this world so as to make them pass through to the next world with the utmost dispatch. 'They teach their children to cry!' was the indignant remark of an Indian woman when confronted with the sanitary separation of mother and child in the government hospital, and especially with the edict of government nurses and doctors that it was good for babies to cry until blue in the face."[2]

In the old Sioux social order, "the baby's nursing was so important that, in principle at least, not even the father's sexual privileges were allowed to interfere with the mother's libidinal concentration on the nursing. A baby's diarrhea was said to be the result of a watery condition of the mother's milk brought about by intercourse with the father. The husband was urged to keep

[1]Erikson, *Childhood and Society.*
[2]Ibid., p. 111.

away from the wife for the nursing period."[3] The average nursing period, it is said, was about three years, and among the old Sioux there was no systematic weaning.

On the other hand, Erikson writes:

> This paradise of the practically unlimited privilege of the mother's breast also had a forbidden fruit. To be permitted to suckle, the infant had to learn not to bite the breast. Sioux grandmothers recount what trouble they had with their indulged babies when they began to use nipples for the first vigorous biting. They tell with amusement how they would "thump" the baby's head and how he would fly into a wild rage. It is at this point that Sioux mothers used to say what our mothers say so much earlier in their babies' lives: Let him cry, it will make him strong. Good future hunters, especially, could be recognized by the strength of their infantile fury. The Sioux baby, when thus filled with rage, was strapped up to his neck in the cradle board. He could not express his rage by the usual violent motion of the limbs.[4]

Erikson postulates a certain congruence between this form of primal relationship and the social ideals of the Sioux:

> A first impression, then, suggests that the cultural demand for generosity received its early foundation from the privilege of enjoying the nourishment and reassurance emanating from unlimited breast feeding; while the necessity of suppressing the biting rage contributed to the tribe's always ready ferocity in that this rage was stored up, channelized, and diverted toward prey and enemy.[5]

Naturally, the training for a society's desired behavioral norms is reinforced during a child's later development by example, sanction and specific initiation rites. But the primal relationship appears to be a basic prerequisite.

In contrast to the nomadic Sioux, the members of the Yurok tribe lived as fishermen in a narrowly circumscribed area along the banks of the salmon-rich Klamath River, which empties into the Pacific on the California coast. Within the framework of this sedentary existence,

[3]Ibid., p. 119.
[4]Ibid., p. 120.
[5]Ibid., p. 121.

The acquisition and retention of possessions is and was what the
Yurok thinks about, talks about and prays for. Every person, every
relationship, and every act can be exactly valued . . . . The Yurok
speak of "clean" living, not of "strong" living, as do the Sioux.
Purity consists of continuous avoidance of impure contacts and
contaminations, and of constant purification from possible contaminations. Having had intercourse with a woman . . . a fisherman must pass the "test" of the sweathouse [and] conclude the
purification by swimming in the river . . . Salmon and the river
dislike it if anything is eaten on a boat. Urine must not enter the
river . . . Salmon demands that women on their trip up or down
river keep special observances, for they may be menstruating.[6]

Seeming almost like an archaic precursor of European puritanism,
these Yurok observances "in reality are folkways of stinginess,
suspicion and anger."[7]

In the realm of infant training, Erikson reports the following:

The newborn is not breast-fed for ten days, but is given a nut soup
from a tiny shell. The breast-feeding begins with Indian generosity
and frequency. However, unlike the Sioux, the Yurok have a
definite weaning time around the sixth month—that is, around the
teething period: a minimal breast-feeding period for American In-
dians. Weaning is called "forgetting the mother" and, if necessary,
is enforced toward the end of the first year by the mother's going
away for a few days . . . The attempt at accelerating autonomy by
early weaning seems to be a part of a general tendency to encourage the baby to leave the mother and her support as soon as
this is possible and bearable . . . From the twentieth day on [the
baby's legs] are massaged by the grandmother to encourage early
creeping. The parents' cooperation in this matter is assured by the
rule that they may resume intercourse when the baby makes
vigorous strides in creeping . . .

The Yurok child is exposed to early and, if necessary, abrupt
weaning before or right after the development of the biting stage,
and this after being discouraged by a number of devices from feeling too comfortable in, with and around his mother. He is to be
trained to be a fisherman: one who has his nets ready for a prey
which (if only he behaves nicely and says "please" appropriately)
comes to him. This fervent attitude of wanting to say "please" to

[6]Ibid., pp. 142, 143.
[7]Ibid., p. 144.

the supernatural providers seems to be reinforced by a residue of infantile nostalgia. The good Yurok is characterized by an ability to cry while he prays in order to gain influence over the food-sending powers beyond the visible world.[8]

In brief, the Yurok were a people among whom "all 'wishful thinking' was put in the service of economic pursuits."[9] Had their early infantile needs been too easily and fully satisfied, too much energy might have been drained from their later concentration on the sources of food. The loss of the maternal breast during the early biting phase thus seems to be linked imaginally with possible loss of the salmon supply from beyond the horizon, an event which must be prevented by all possible means, including magic. Erikson sums up:

> Thus they felt secure in a system of avoidances: avoidance of being drawn into a fight, into a contamination, into a bad business deal. Their individual lives began with an early banishment from the mother's breast, and with subsequent instruction (for boys) to avoid her, to keep out of her living quarters, and to beware of snaring women in general. Their mythology banishes the creator from this world by having him snared and abducted by a woman. While the fear of being caught thus dominated their avoidances, they lived every moment for the purpose of snatching an advantage from another human being.[10]

Every analyst is familiar with the Yurok pattern as it applies to people with a negative mother complex and the resulting existential anxieties, which are overcompensated by many of the attitudes and symptoms decribed.

Other archaic groups have been studied by Margaret Mead[11] (between 1925 and 1933) and more recently by the psychoanalysts Parin, Morgenthaler and Parin-Matthey.[12] In every case clear links have been observed between post-natal mothering, early

[8]Ibid., pp. 150–151.
[9]Ibid., p. 152.
[10]Ibid., p. 155.
[11]*Sex and Temperament in Three Primitive Societies*. New York: William Morrow & Co., 1963.
[12]P. Parin, F. Morgenthaler, and G. Parin-Matthey, *Fear Thy Neighbor As Thyself: Psychoanalysis and Society Among the Anyi of West Africa*. Chicago: University of Chicago Press, 1980; *Die Weissen denken zu viel* (White Men Think Too Much). Munich: Kindler Taschenbuch 2079 o.J.

child-rearing practices, and patterns of adult social behavior. With
the aid of regular, psychoanalytically oriented talks with individuals, Parin and Morgenthaler also gained insight into some generally obscure areas of perception and conflict among some of the
tribesmen.

It is worth noting that among such peaceable planters as the
Mountain Arapesh of New Guinea (Mead) and the Dogon in West
Africa (Parin), maternal care and attention are given in abundance.
According to Mead, it is typical of the social behavior of the rather
poor Arapesh that cooperation is regarded as the highest value.
They do not see their land as belonging to them; rather, they
belong to it. The true owners are the ancestral spirits. Mead points
out that this is "a social order that substitutes responsiveness to
the concerns of others, and attentiveness to the needs of others,
for aggressiveness, initiative, competitiveness and possessiveness
—the familiar motivations upon which our culture depends."[13]

Planting gardens, hunting for kangaroo and smaller game,
building houses, all such activities are performed in volunteer
groups. "But this loosely cooperative fashion in which all work
is organized means that no man is master of his own plans for
many hours together . . . The men spend over nine-tenths of their
time responding to other people's plans, digging in other people's
gardens, going on hunting parties initiated by others."[14] No one
harvests or hunts for himself alone. These people have confidence
that they will never be left in the lurch by their society. The arts
of warfare are virtually unknown and he who kills someone is
regarded with considerable malaise by his fellow tribesmen. In
other words, this society lives out a kind of "communism" that
requires no administrative or bureaucratic apparatus, since the
danger of isolation is enough to guarantee the cooperation of each
individual. Despite their poverty, the Arapesh are a cheerful
people.

The father shares responsibility for providing the Arapesh baby
with good mothering. He "lies quietly beside his newborn child,
from time to time giving the mother little bits of advice . . . From
time to time they perform small, magical rites that will ensure the
child's welfare and their ability to care for it."[15] A man who has

[13]*Sex and Temperament in Three Primitive Societies*, p. 15.
[14]Ibid., p. 22.
[15]Ibid., p. 34.

become a father for the first time, after spending five days in total isolation with his wife and child, undergoes a kind of initiation ceremony performed by a godfather. "The ceremony might be said to symbolize the regaining of the father's masculine nature after his important share in feminine functions."[16] The father, however, continues to spend every night with his wife and child, though all sexual activity is taboo—even with another wife, if he has one. Even extramarital sex is considered dangerous until the child has taken its first steps.

This sexual abstinence is practiced mainly for the benefit of the child, partly to make sure that it will not have to be weaned too suddenly and too soon because of the arrival of another infant. Obviously, parental care and self-sacrifice are highly developed here. A child is never left alone, and is given the breast as soon as it cries. Mead states that "nursing is, for mother and child, one long delightful and highly charged game, in which the easy, warm affectivity of a lifetime is set up."[17]

According to the Dogon people, as reported by Parin and Morgenthaler,[18] Paradise differs from reality only in that its gardens are even greener and its fruit more brilliant. Among them, too, the true owners of the soil are the spirits of those who have lived on it before. These spirits are not really feared, but an appropriate sacrifice must be made to them at harvest time. The investigators found very little fear among the Dogon adults in general, since each individual feels thoroughly contained in the community. They also found surprisingly few disturbances of the vegetative system. As is the case among the Arapesh, the individual Dogon does not develop a distinctly separate and autonomous ego identity. Here, individual conscience is identical with clan conscience[19]; this is derived from the group, which in turn makes its standards felt by a combination of rewards and direct pressure.

Summing up, Parin and Morgenthaler state:

> The Dogon are infused with great confidence that all wishes can be fulfilled. Their optimism appears to us unshakable and unrealistic, formed through their long experience of containment with the mother and confirmed by the subsequent containment

[16]Ibid., p. 35.
[17]Ibid., p. 43.
[18]*Die Weissen denken zu viel* (White Men Think Too Much).
[19]Ibid., p. 437.

in the social environment. A Dogon can hardly be disappointed in love. If a man simply finds a wife and she has a child, his principal wishes are thus fulfilled. Happiness is endangered only through loss of the loved one or through external misfortune . . . Though the Dogon are more vulnerable to external dangers than people of the West, they experience less anxiety. Though they are more dependent on their environment, they are less lonely. They are less prone to repress inner conflicts, and get along with their fellows better than we do.[20]

Dogon mothers nurse their children for between two and three years. The children are given much love, are caressed and carried a great deal. At any sign of discomfort, they are immediately given the breast. Weaning comes suddenly. But by then the youngsters also have grown accustomed to eating porridge, and they continue to be given all the treats they want until they are about seven years old. There is no special toilet training prior to weaning. Older children then serve as role models in learning to master the excretory functions. After being weaned, a child is cared for largely by siblings and other children of the extended family, who generally lavish a great deal of care and attention upon it.

Margaret Mead encountered an entirely different situation among the cannibal River Mundugumor in New Guinea. The Mundugumor are prosperous, enjoying an abundance of fertile land and waters rich in fish. Most work is done by the women, giving the men ample time to act out their hostilities. There is no communal men's house among the Mundugumor, since these men live in constant fear and mistrust of one another. That is why each surrounds his territory with a high fence behind which, for reasons of prestige, are the lodgings of as many wives as possible. Daughters must be carefully guarded, since they have an exchange value for their brothers, who can use them as compensation when acquiring wives for themselves. As a result, daughters are frequently abducted. "Mundugumor social organization is based on a theory of a natural hostility that exists between all members of the same sex, and the assumption that the only possible ties between members of the same sex are through members of the opposite sex."[21]

---

[20]Ibid., pp. 461–462.
[21]*Sex and Temperament in Three Primitive Societies*, p. 176.

Pregnancy and birth are apparently highly unwelcome among the Mundugumor because they force the temporary cessation of sexual relations. Consequently, newborn sons are sometimes killed. Daughters are preferred for their exchange value, especially by the fathers, and therefore tend to be kept alive. Infants are placed in a narrow, woven carrying basket. When a baby cries, it is not taken to the breast immediately. Its mother, or someone in the vicinity, merely establishes contact by scratching the infant's basket with a fingernail.

> Mundugumor women suckle their children standing up, supporting the child with one hand in a position that strains the mother's arm and pinions the arms of the child. There is none of the mother's dallying, sensuous pleasure in feeding her child that occurs among the Arapesh. Nor is the child permitted to prolong his meal by any playful fondling of his own or his mother's body. He is kept firmly to his major task of absorbing enough food so that he will stop crying and consent to be put back in his basket. The minute he stops suckling for a moment he is returned to his prison. Children therefore develop a very definite, purposive fighting attitude, holding on firmly to the nipple and sucking milk as rapidly and vigorously as possible. They frequently choke from swallowing too fast; the choking angers the mother and infuriates the child, thus further turning the suckling situation into one characterized by anger and struggle rather than by affection and reassurance.[22]

Weaning is accomplished brutally, with a smack whenever the child tries to reach for the mother's breast. The Mundugumor treat all illnesses and accidents, even among little children, as "matters for exasperation and anger, as if the personality of the parent were invaded and insulted by the illness of the child."[23]

Given these methods, only the strongest children survive, the ones who can learn to adjust to the rough ways of a hostile world. Mead reports that "the Mundugumor idea of character is identical for the two sexes . . . . both men and women are expected to be violent, competitive, aggressively sexed, jealous and ready to see and avenge insult, delighting in display, in action, in fighting. The Mundugumor have selected as their ideal the very types of men

[22]Ibid., pp. 195–196.
[23]Ibid., p. 196.

and women which the Arapesh consider to be so incomprehensible that they hardly allow for their occurrence.''[24]

The situation is not quite as dramatic among the Anyi of Africa's Ivory Coast, as studied and reported upon by Parin and Morgenthaler in their book *Fear Thy Neighbor As Thyself*. The Anyi enjoy a proud tradition as a prosperous and warlike people, having been in the past aristocratic, large-scale landowners. Unlike the Dogon, who

> never resort to constraint in politics or pedagogy, the Anyi, by contrast, achieve their social goals almost exclusively by constraint, fear, and punishment. We never heard a child crying for any length of time in a Dogon village; someone always hurried to comfort it. Our stay in Bébou [the Anyi village in which the authors lived], on the other hand, was an ordeal simply because of the incessant, heartrending sobbing of the children, day and night.[25]
>
> Direct observation of a number of infants revealed surprisingly small variations in the behavior of the mothers. Throughout infancy, the child stays close to his mother. At night he sleeps naked next to her naked body on a mat or bed, the two of them covered by the same cotton blanket. During the day the mother carries him on her back.[26]

It is noteworthy that the Anyi mother, when nursing, assumes a position which makes it impossible for the baby to establish eye contact with her. Nor does she speak a word to the child or react to any sounds it may make, and during the long hours that she spends dreaming in the shade with her baby, she often sits "staring depressively at nothing."[27]

Beginning just a few days after birth, Anyi babies receive one or two enemas daily, prepared with a suspension of ground chili peppers, immediately after which they are placed between the mother's knees on a toilet pot. The infants twist and turn as if they had stomach-ache, but they neither struggle nor cry. The practice of administering enemas is continued throughout the life of the Anyi, who are addicted to them. Parin and Morgenthaler in-

[24]Ibid., p. 225.
[25]Parin, Morgenthaler, and Parin-Matthey, *Fear Thy Neighbor As Thyself: Psychoanalysis and Society Among the Anyi of West Africa*, pp. 6–7.
[26]Ibid., p. 134.
[27]Ibid., pp. 134, 135.

terpret this to mean that the Anyi deeply mistrust the contents of their bodies and therefore try to get rid of them as quickly as possible. (It should be added here that many European and American mothers still swear by this "method." In my practice I have observed that children treated in this way experience enemas as a physical violation and tend toward masochistic, submissive behavior as adults. They are highly mistrustful of whatever they wish to express verbally or emotionally, as if they feel that they have no right to their own "insides." At the same time, analysis reveals a great deal of repressed anger and sadistic fantasies, with sexual desires and imaginings concentrating strongly on the anal zone.)

Weaning among the Anyi occurs suddenly and radically after about 18 months. The mother continues to feed the child and tend to its bodily needs, but otherwise ignores it completely. She regards it as no longer her child; it has already become too independent. At this point the mother's desire is for another infant with which she can gratify her own instinctual needs. From here on, the child receives only commands and punishments, combined with threats and blows. Every older child can order a younger one around; the younger are completely at the mercy of the older children's superior strength.

The consequence of all this is that, even among Anyi adults, fear and fury constitute an emotional potential which may break out at any time from behind the social façade of stiff and proper etiquette. The deep-seated mistrust which is rife in the psyches of these people is illustrated, among other things, by the fact that nearly every instance of death in their territory is ascribed by the Anyi to malicious action by someone else rather than to natural causes. The belief in evil witches is one of the worst plagues besetting this tribe. The Anyi also find it virtually impossible to engage in lasting love relationships. One of their great pieces of tribal wisdom says: "Follow your heart and you perish."[28]

Before closing this chapter mention should be made of the work of F. Renggli,[29] whose studies of several archaic societies provide detailed portrayals of the socio-cultural consequences of the mother-child relationship during the first year of a child's life.

[28]Ibid., p. 388.
[29]F. Renggli, *Angst und Geborgenheit* (Fear and Security).

8. Primal Relationship and Cultural Canon in the History of European Parent-Child Relations

Our brief excursion into the mores of various primitive peoples certainly lent support to the hypothesis that there are links between a society's predominant form of primal relationship and its collective social behavior. The mother archetype is apparently constellated in a variety of ways throughout the socio-cultural field of which child-rearing is an integral part. Among the Arapesh and the Dogon it is clearly the "positive elementary character of the Great Mother"[1] which predominates, with measurable effects not only on the behavior of each individual mother but also on the cultural canon of the entire tribe. Among the Mundugumor and, to a lesser degree, among the Anyi, the image of the "Terrible Mother" is clearly in the ascendant and the world is perceived primarily as the hostile environment mother, evoking constant mistrust and guardedness in each individual.

Yet it is far too simple to assume a direct causal relationship, to assert that because mothers behave in a generally loving or in a generally cruel way toward their children the results are specific aspects of an entire tribe's social behavior together with a particular world-view. There is a recurring but fruitless dispute among psychologists as to whether a certain type of child-rearing gives rise to a particular culture or whether, on the contrary, it

[1]Neumann, *The Great Mother*.

is the culture which determines the type of child-rearing. "It has often enough been shown that child-rearing practices provide the foundation for the adult personality. But every psychoanalyst who has posed it, has been embarrassed by the question of the origin of those practices."[2]

What we are dealing with here is the fundamental question of how a society acquires its particular *Weltanschauung* and human ideals. As we have seen, Erik Erikson, to take one example, has tried to view maternal behavior within the context of a given group's vital activities. A nomadic, adventuresome, prairie-dwelling buffalo hunter will of necessity have characteristics and ideals quite different from those of a sedentary fisherman living along the banks of a salmon-filled river. To a certain extent this looks like a kind of economic determinism, although Erikson does not intend it in the true Marxist sense.

Renggli, too, speaks of "survival value," the necessary adjustments made by a society to the ecological realities of its situation. Using a number of examples he demonstrates how changes in those environmental realities are accompanied by alterations in behavioral values. And with these come shifts in child-rearing, changes which constitute necessary adaptations to the new circumstances if the society is to survive. "The treatment of children and ecological or economic realities thus constitute a reciprocal system, that is, changes in one always result in changes in the other."[3]

Ultimately, however, the question of how diverse world-views and human ideals originate touches on the mystery of the spiritual components of human existence—reason enough for the embarrassment of those who try to answer that question. Renggli believes that, from his biological perspective, he can provide a definition of culture, an explanation for why the behavioral patterns of a particular people are formed and institutionalized in a particular way:

> A culture, so I believe, is an attempt to resolve those conflicts and fears which have been inevitably generated by a specific mother-child relationship during the first year of life, and thus by a specific

[2]L. de Mause, *Hört ihr die Kinder weinen* (Hear the Children Crying). Frankfurt/M: Suhrkamp, 1977, pp. 13–14.
[3]*Angst und Geborgenheit* (Fear and Security), p. 242.

technique of child-rearing, which is itself an ecological adjustment.
In this way the individual adult is relieved of the necessity of per-
sonally working through his own anxieties.[4]

This is certainly a plausible interpretation, in part. But it presupposes the primacy of the specific mother-child relation.

Somehow the entire discussion is reminiscent of the old dispute
over which came first, the chicken or the egg. In the final analysis
human culture, with all its variations, possibilities and terrors, is
based on mankind's creative unconscious, which constitutes in
itself an irreducible, archetypal *a priori*. The contours of a particular cultural canon, however, are certainly dependent upon
which archetypal configurations are constellated. And that constellation is frequently the psyche's response to environmental
realities and, of course, also to the early mother-child relation.

Even more clearly than Renggli, de Mause postulates a "psycho-
genetic theory of history" which starts from the premise "that the
central, driving force of historical change is to be found neither
in technology nor in the economy, but rather in the 'psycho-
genic' changes in the structure of personality and character
which result from the interaction between parents and children
in the course of the generations."[5] His book, written in collaboration with other psychoanalytically schooled authors, does not initially set out to prove this theory. Its more modest goal is "to
reconstruct, on the basis of available testimony, what it has meant
in the past to be a child or a parent."[6]

The work confines itself to depicting the history of childhood
in Europe since the late Roman era. For the most part the testimony reveals a tale of suffering: infanticide, abandonment, sale,
neglect, sexual abuse, barbaric diapering practices, deliberate star-
vation, beating, isolation. The child's dependence on adult care
has opened the door to every kind of tyranny. It was not until the
year 374 A.D. that the killing of a child was regarded as murder
under the law.

Infanticide was not illegal before that time; in fact, in the two
centuries after Augustus an effort was made to pay parents to let

[4]Ibid.
[5]L. de Mause, *Hört ihr die Kinder weinen* (Hear the Children Crying), p. 14.
[6]Ibid., p. 15.

their children live, in order to halt the decline of Rome's population.[7] De Mause comments: "What parents of the past lacked was not love, but the emotional maturity necessary to acknowledge that a child is a human being in its own right."[8] This level of maturity requires the "empathic reaction," the ability to feel one's way into the world of the small child and its particular needs. This presupposes a rather highly developed faculty of differentiation, capable of separating one's own person, expectations, ideas and needs, from those of the child. The author writes: "It is difficult to estimate what proportion of parents have attained this level of empathy with any consistency even today."[9] Every analyst can share this uncertainty, on the basis of clinical experience.

According to the copious documentation presented in this book, until well into the 18th century that level of differentiated consciousness had not yet been developed in parents, with very few exceptions. Parents unconsciously drew children into their own psychic world, using them as screens on which to project the contents of their own unconscious. Seen from this perspective, the child emerges as a figure consisting of the projected wishes, hostilities, anxieties and sexual fantasies of adults.

The belief, for example, that children could at any moment transform themselves into totally godless creatures, was a major reason why they were kept tied in place or tightly bound throughout so much of history. An endless variety of corsets, "safety" lines, backboards, etc., was devised to prevent children from crawling around on the ground "like animals."

All of this involves the "God-willed" repression of man's animal nature, lived out projectively in children. De Mause draws a distinction between this "projective reaction" and what he calls the "reverse reaction," which is what occurs when parents use their children as a substitute for an adult figure. In the reverse reaction the child is perceived as being there only to serve the needs of the parents. A modern mother with a child abuse problem once expressed it this way: "I've never felt loved in all my

[7]Ibid., p. 50.
[8]Ibid., p. 35.
[9]Ibid.

life. When the baby came I thought it would love me. When it screamed, that meant it didn't love me. That's why I beat it."[10]

De Mause has divided parent-child relations in the course of European history into six forms or categories, developing progressively toward the capacity for empathic parental behavior. He remarks, however, that the historical periods and behavioral patterns he has enumerated apply in each case only to the psychogenetically most advanced segment of the populace in the most advanced countries. (Even today, as has recently become amply clear, children are still being killed, beaten and sexually abused.)

The following historical categorization of parent-child relations seems to me quite instructive and illuminating with regard to maternal behavior today. "Historical" forms of behavior never completely disappear, of course; they continue to exist subliminally in the unconscious.

1. *Infanticide* (Antiquity to 4th Century A.D.). Parents are legally able to escape from their own parental anxieties by exposing their children to the elements, throwing them into the Tiber or finding some other way of killing them. The projective reaction is overwhelmingly predominant.

2. *Abandonment* (4th to 13th Century A.D.). Parents recognize that children have a soul. But projection is still strong; the child is full of evil and must be beaten. The best solution is seen as giving the child away—to a wet nurse, a monastery, foster parents, as a servant or hostage to an aristocratic family. At home, children are often abandoned to complete emotional isolation.

3. *Ambivalence* (14th to 17th Century). It is thought that a child is made of some pliable substance (like wax, plaster, clay) and must be molded to the proper form, both mentally and physically. The emotional relationship between parents and children becomes more personal, but this serves to intensify parental ambivalence between love and rejection. From the 14th century onward there is a growing body of advice and instruction on child-rearing, as well as greater spread of the Madonna and Child cult with its attendant image of the "passionate mother."

4. *Intrusion*. (18th Century). Parents attempt to penetrate the child's inner space—not only physically, with the enema, but "to

[10]Ibid., p. 20.

penetrate its spirit, in order to bring its anger, its needs, its mastur-
bation, indeed its will, under control. The child raised by intrusive
parents was nursed by its mother, was not given enemas regularly, was toilet trained early, prayed with the others instead of
playing with them, was beaten but no longer regularly whipped,
was punished for masturbating and was trained to prompt obedience by means of threats, guilt feelings and other kinds of
punishment."[11] At the same time, empathy begins to develop,
since the child is no longer perceived as such a threat. There are
the beginnings of pediatric medicine and a general improvement
in parental care, resulting in a decline in child mortality.

5. *Socialization* (19th to mid 20th Century). Due to a further
diminution of emotion-laden projections, child-rearing no longer
consists primarily of subjugating the child's will. Attention is concentrated on preparing the child for the "struggle for survival,"
educating it, helping it to adjust, putting it on the right path,
socializing it. "Most people today still regard socialization as the
only model of child-training on the basis of which a discussion
of child care can be pursued. It is the origin of all twentieth-
century psychological models, from Freud's 'repression of instinct' to Skinner's behaviorism."[12] The increased interest of the
father in the education and training of his children also has its
beginnings in the 19th century.

6. *Support* (from the mid-20th Century). "The supportive form
of relationship is based on the view that the child knows better
than its parents what it needs in each stage of its life. This type
of relationship draws both parents into the life of the child; they
try to feel their way into the child's expanding and specific needs
and to fulfill them." Under this system children are no longer
beaten or berated, and their parents (or teachers) apologize if they
have yelled at them under stress. The supportive relationship
demands from both parents an extraordinary amount of time,
energy and willingness to discuss, particularly during the first six
years of a child's life. Quite obviously we are dealing here with
what is commonly known as anti-authoritarian upbringing, which
de Mause advocates wholeheartedly. He writes: "Up to now only

[11]Ibid., p. 84.
[12]Ibid.

a small number of parents have tried to care for their children in this way. But the four books[13] which describe children who have grown up within the supportive form of relationship clearly show that within such a framework children develop who are friendly, honest, not depressive, who do not constantly imitate others, are not exclusively group-oriented, have a strong will and are not intimidated by authority."[14]

Although it may be somewhat skewed on the negative side, this historical overview of parent-child relations in European society stimulates speculation about possible links between early mother-child relations, cultural structures and social behavior. In their book de Mause and his colleagues do not venture any conclusions with reference to society as a whole. But in a purely speculative vein I make no secret of my own impression that many facts seem to support the hypothesis of such links.

For example, in the face of all Christian exhortations to "love thy neighbor," our history is marked by a high degree of militant aggressivity. During the Middle Ages, moreover, earthly existence was experienced largely as a "vale of sorrows," human nature was regarded as *a priori* evil, plagued by Original Sin. (This may be an indication of the kind of "primary guilt" we have seen to be characteristic of a disturbed primal relationship.) There was a powerful longing for redemption in the Hereafter. And there was a most blatant split of the mother archetype into a higher, spiritualized aspect and a lower, dark, feared, "bad," instinct-nature aspect. The worship of the Madonna revolves around a mother-figure that has never been touched by earthly sexuality. This in itself expresses a split between Eros and Sexus. Even the beloved, revered lady of the medieval troubadors was not the object of sexual desire.

Instinctual sexuality was seen as evil and projected onto "witches," where it was persecuted. In the work known as the *Malleus Maleficarum* ("The Witches' Hammer"), which was composed in 1487 by two Dominican monks and served as a basis for

---

[13]A. S. Neill, *The Free Child*, London, 1952; P. and J. Ritter, *Freie Kindererziehung in der Familie* (Free Childrearing in the Family). Reinbek: Rowohlt, 1972; M. Deakin, *The Children on the Hill*. London: 1972; and L. de Mause, a book about his son (not yet published).

[14]L. de Mause, *Hört ihr die Kinder weinen* (Hear the Children Crying), p. 85.

the witch hunts of the Inquisition, sexual motivations emerge with remarkable clarity. In addition to the sexual, the entire arsenal of fantasies and images linked to the archetype of the "Terrible Goddess" was projected onto those poor women chosen to play the witch's role.

Another facet of life in the Middle Ages was the lack of empathy between man and woman. "There were many obstacles to the establishment of sensitive sympathy with women in the West, and to a great extent this is still the case today . . . Love remained copulation, no more. There was no genuine familiarity with women." With these words A. and W. Leibbrand close their chapter on "The Discovery of Love" in their examination of the phenomenon of the medieval Provençal troubadors.[15] The Church had declared all of these things to be immoral.

On the other hand, European history has also been a succession of religious, intellectual, creative-artistic and scientific attainments, revealing the heights and depths of psychic dimensions. The inhabitants of Huxley's Brave New World, by contrast, can do no more than giggle at Shakespeare, having absolutely no comprehension of his depth. To Freud, of course, human culture was based on the painful repression of instinctual drives.

In any case, it is evident that the most profound ideas and greatest creative achievements of which mankind is capable are grounded in the vulnerability of human existence to the experience of suffering and anxiety. The greatest cultural achievements appear to be attempts at dealing meaningfully with human suffering. To what extent the attainments of culture past and present, including our increasingly differentiated consciousness and individualization, may be a direct result of a fruitful working-through of such primal suffering, is a question which naturally cannot be answered in general terms. But the biographies of many geniuses seem to point in that direction. Certainly the possibility of such links cannot be dismissed, although in themselves they can never suffice to "explain" the complexity of human nature and human culture.

[15]A. and W. Leibbrand, *Formen des Eros* (Forms of Eros), Vol. I. Freiburg & Munich: Alber, 1972, p. 626.

9. Infant Care and Group Behavior in the Israeli Kibbutz

Before turning our attention to some practical implications of today's mother-child situation, I should like to examine another model of child rearing: the practice of collective upbringing in the Israeli kibbutz. The child psychologist Bruno Bettelheim has published a highly readable study on this subject.[1]

Kibbutz is the Hebrew word for "group." The founders of the kibbutzim in Palestine wanted to create a new form of social life based upon socialist ideals. While they were influenced by the *Wandervogel* movement's revolt against the authoritarian family and the repressive demands of European civilization, according to Bettelheim, "the manner in which they combined it [the *Wandervogel* ideology] with socialism, Zionism and a Tolstoyan emphasis on the virtues of life on the land, was uniquely their own."[2]

In the *shtetl*, the ghetto communities of their mostly East European homelands, life was concentrated largely on the family. As a consequence, the early Jewish pioneers did not want to include a conventional family structure in the new social form they were striving to create. Above all, in contrast to traditional role distribution, women were to enjoy full equality with men in the kibbutz. This was a revolutionary concept, especially when one considers that in Orthodox Judaism men are enjoined to thank God each

[1]*Children of the Dream*. New York: The Macmillan Company, 1969.
[2]Ibid., p. 21.

day that "Thou hast not created me as a woman." Furthermore, the thoughts of the often bitterly poor ghetto families of Eastern Europe had revolved incessantly around religious values and material possessions. In a compensatory development, the idea arose that life in the kibbutz would include neither religion nor materialism. Private property would be abolished; everything would belong to the collective.[3]

It is against this background that kibbutz child-rearing must be examined. Bettelheim offers some interesting remarks on the psychology of the founding women of the kibbutz movement: "To the founding woman, her mother's life seemed so overwhelming an example of giving to children, so much all of one piece, that she could not imagine herself identifying with part of it, and not others. These mothers of theirs, in their single-minded devotion to family and children, seemed most powerful figures to their daughters. To be free of such an image, one had to be free of it *in toto*."[4]

In other words, woman as man's comrade and equal partner could not at the same time be a good mother; her own inner image of "Mother" made too many demands to permit this. Bettelheim states:

> Often it took little probing to elicit this feeling in some women: They had feared being totally inadequate as mothers, particularly with their firstborn. In some cases, where I could penetrate more deeply, the other aspect became apparent as well: They felt deeply guilty about the radical rejection of their mothers' readiness to make sacrifices for children. All this remained thinly disguised behind rationalizations: By true kibbutz values, only physical labor in the fields was worthwhile; they could not afford to neglect their labors by devoting too much time to their children.[5]

At the same time there was a widespread conviction that collective child-rearing was better for the child than individual mothering and the family setting. "The insistence that all emotional disturbance is caused by the parents and none by kibbutz rear-

[3]It should be pointed out here that religious kibbutzim were subsequently also founded and that many of the original ideas and principles of kibbutz life were later modified.
[4]Bettelheim, *Children of the Dream*, p. 31.
[5]Ibid., pp. 33–34.

ing, suggests that bad mothering, or parenthood, is viewed as the only possible cause of emotional maladjustment."[6]

A newborn child was kept in the infants' house from the outset, where it was visited by its mother for nursing purposes for a maximum period of six months. (Nursing was regarded as the "natural" way to feed an infant.) After this time, generally, it was weaned. In addition, as soon as possible the infant began to be fed by the *metapelet*, the nurse in charge of the infants' house, not from a bottle but, beginning at four months of age, from a cup. Bettelheim ascribes a number of motives to this early weaning. One of them is that the mother wanted to be free to return to her kibbutz work as soon as possible. But not all mothers find their work more rewarding than the time they spend with their baby. There was also the consideration of "collective justice," which dictated that all children should be nursed for more or less the same length of time.[7]

The fact that the mother is present only sporadically means that the mutual tie between mother and infant does not become so intense. Similarly, the *metapelet*, the nurse in charge, is not always present, with the night shift often being handled by a steady succession of persons. As a result, the strongest emotional attachment from quite an early age onward tends to be with the peer group, the makeup of which remains constant. Says Bettelheim:

> Much more important in time and emotional impact are the constant companions who live in [the baby's] room. Them he always sees and reacts to . . . Separation anxiety in the kibbutz is thus very typically experienced around the absence of a peer. And it can never be felt as acutely as by the middle class infant whose mother leaves him, because however important the infant in the next crib, he is not the only one in the room, nor the only one life revolves around.[8]

It cannot be maintained that the people of the kibbutz-born generation suffer from a disturbance of their "basic trust," since

[6]Ibid., p. 33.
[7]According to my own information, these matters are handled more flexibly and individually in some kibbutzim today. Some mothers now insist that their infant be allowed to sleep in the parents' apartment, and here too the kibbutz collective is often not as rigid as it used to be.
[8]*Children of the Dream,* p. 86.

the archetypal "environment mother," experienced as a combination of the peer group, the *metapelet* and the personal mother, provides a constant sense of security. In addition to its own mother, the other infants and their mothers, as well as the *metapelet* and her helpers, all belong to the more or less constant inventory of the kibbutz baby's life.

Bettelheim remarks on this:

> So while the kibbutz child may fare less well, compared with a child among us who has an excellent mother-infant relationship, he fares considerably better, for example, than the many infants in our society whose mothers, because of the nature of their own toilet training or for other neurotic reasons, find the child's excreta repulsive; or than those infants whose mothers make of bathing an essentially arduous task of getting the infant clean, a task often performed with compulsive rigidity, or else in a hurry because other things need attending. In the kibbutz the infant nurse has at least received some instruction on how to take care of infants.[9]

Among the members of the kibbutz-born generation, Bettelheim found identification of the individual with group consciousness and its value hierarchies. Impulses of an individual and personal nature tend to be repressed in favor of internalized group demands. And it is not only close parental ties, with their attendant conflicts, that are avoided from the outset; the young person's search for the intimate friendship of "soulmates" is likewise blocked by the group, because such relationships tend toward exclusivity. "Not only is a relative isolation completely out of reach, but so is any intimate friendship, because the group always intrudes."[10] Very little opportunity is provided for discovery of the dimension of psychic inwardness. After the 1967 Six Day War, one kibbutznik expressed his reactions in this striking fashion:

> "It forced us to think. Types like us don't really know how to ruminate about problems of good and bad, justice and injustice, about what is permissible and what is forbidden. Within the framework of our way of life, we are generally not the type of people who go into depth in matters of soul searching . . . The group of us now have some contact with our feelings, are asking

[9]Ibid., p. 120.
[10]Ibid., pp. 233–234.

whether things are right or wrong, all as a result of the battles. It's
a pity we achieved this only through the war experience, but it's
good that it motivates us to do a bit of soul-searching."[11]

As contained and secure as the individual may feel in this collective life-style, on closer questioning it turned out that many kibbutzniks suffered from having to be constantly at the group's
disposal and always under someone's eye.

Bettelheim noted an interesting psychological phenomenon:
Many kibbutzniks, especially men, had developed an intense love
for a particular piece of land in the vicinity of their settlement.
One young fellow, for example, would spend fourteen and more
hours a day herding sheep, often seven days a week, because the
work gave him the chance to be alone in his favorite spot.
Another man had a wife who was determined to leave their kibbutz, so that their children could live at home, but although he
was a good father and husband (according to his wife's
testimony), he could not bring himself to leave the small lake
where he spent almost all his days—not because of the fishing,
but because of the lake's beauty. Apparently it was only in Nature's company that these (and other) kibbutzniks had the feeling that it was permissible to be alone and drawn inward, and that
they were not missing anything in the absence of their comrades.
Compensation was apparently provided by the need for a bit of
paradisial landscape.

In discussing this phenomenon, Bettelheim comments that he
was forced time and again to think of the phrase "Mother Earth,"
as though the native-born kibbutznik were searching for a kind
of unqualified acceptance without any commitment in return,
something that he had never known in his childhood because acceptance as a small child was always tied to the demands of collective life.

In his book Bettelheim points up yet another special problem
of the kibbutz: The founding generation of the kibbutz movement
consisted largely of creative, European-raised, strongly individual
personalities, including some of the most important leaders of the
young State of Israel. To create a new life-style and a better society
called for a pioneering spirit and a rebellious attitude toward tradi-

[11]Ibid., p. 258.

tional forms. But once the kibbutz had been created and was accepted by a majority of its members, the spirit of rebellion was no longer desirable and would have seriously disrupted the system. Thus the second generation of native-born kibbutzniks differs from the founder generation, in that group identity is the outstanding psychological hallmark of the former, with the development of specific individuality very much recessive.

Summing up, Bettelheim comments:

> Perhaps the assets and liabilities of kibbutz education may best be summarized by the deep peer attachments felt by the second generation. On the one hand, their reluctance to contemplate a life apart from each other, the way each one, alone, seems to feel things only half as acutely as when all function together as a unit—all these seem to speak more of bondage than attachment. (Though what is bondage in one society may be experienced very differently in another.) On the other hand, if intense group ties discourage individuation, neither do they breed human isolation, asocial behavior or other forms of social disorganization that plague modern man in competitive society.[12]

Whatever else it may have done, the experiment of kibbutz life has given the lie to predictions by psychologists and psychiatrists that a system which separates infants from the family, and especially from the mother, and raises them in group homes, must fail catastrophically. This is clearly not the case. That fact is quite explicable from the standpoint of Analytical Psychology: The supporting, nourishing, containing mother of the primal relationship is an archetypal configuration which need not necessarily be identical with the personal mother. The experience of "good enough" mothering as the foundation for "basic trust" can apparently also be supplied by the system practiced in the kibbutzim. At the same time Bettelheim's observations show once again that the manner in which the early archetypal need for mothering is met would seem to favor the imprinting of certain characteristic modes of experience and behavior.

The kibbutz form of child-rearing has been discussed at some length here partly because, among young people of the West, kibbutz society often is the carrier for a projection of the Paradise

[12]Ibid., p. 294.

image. When that happens, the idea of the kibbutz represents the
longing to overcome one's own sense of isolation, to find relief
from one's own sense of responsibility, to be contained in a net-
work of collective meaning and relationship—in brief, the longing for gratification of a frustrated need for "security" in the fully
rounded sense of the term *Geborgenheit*.

10. The Father Archetype as the Basis of Social Norms

Our examination of the interaction between the early mother-child relationship and socio-cultural realities raises some interesting questions about the current situation in Western industrial society.

Erich Neumann proceeds on the assumption that there is a species-appropriate behavior pattern for a mother to follow toward her infant and that a mother can evoke a healthy experience of the primal relationship by relating to her baby as much as possible in tune with her archetypal maternal role, that is, in an instinctively species-appropriate manner. Perhaps what Neumann means is something similar to the inherent, maternal "brood behavior" described among various species, including man, by the ethologist I. Eibl-Eibesfeldt.[1] But our examination of various forms of mother-child relationship has shown that this "natural," instinctive, species-appropriate maternal behavior is a very flexible concept. To an Arapesh mother, for example, the behavior of a Mundugumor mother would be totally unnatural and despicable—and vice versa. We must not forget that part of mankind's species-appropriate nature is imbeddedness in a social fabric and its particular set of cultural norms and value systems. One might say that it is also man's "nature" to be a cultural creature.

The behavior of a mother toward her infant is influenced to a great extent by norms which are in turn based on cultural and

[1] Irenäus Eibl-Eibesfeldt, *Love and Hate: The Natural History of Behavior Patterns.* New York: Holt, Rinehart & Winston, 1972.

81

social value systems. Those norms are, at the very least, intertwined with the biophysical, species-specific behavior constellated by the mother archetype, and may even come into conflict
with it.

Neumann speaks in this context of "the intervention of the
patriarchal principle of order represented by the mother's consciousness and her animi."[2] Neumann characterizes this principle
of order as "patriarchal" regardless of whether the social framework is that of a primitive matriarchy (about which we know very
little) or our Judeo-Christian patriarchy. This is because norms
which channel and limit instinctual human behavior are experienced as expressions of the Logos principle.

Logos is the faculty of differentiating and delimiting subject and
object, which makes possible cognition and analytical thought.
An emotional tie gets in the way of "objective" evaluation of a
person or situation. Love and hate both typically make a person
blind to the realities of other people. Logos as the capacity to differentiate also brings with it a critical capacity (from the Greek *kri-
nein*, "to differentiate"). Are things in nature good as they are,
or could they, indeed *should* they, be otherwise? Human technology, the ability to alter and exploit nature, is as much based
on Logos as are ethical imperatives. The latter are guidelines,
norms, on the basis of which judgments can be made of how
human behavior *ought* to be—which is often in conflict with the
reality of how it is "by nature."

The law-giving principle of order is experienced archetypally
through masculine symbolism. In the psychic realm it is dominated by what C. G. Jung termed the father archetype. At this
point, therefore, we offer a few general observations on the workings of the father archetype and its symbolism—the psychic
source of all that is comprehended by the terms patriarchal and
patriarchy. But first, an important cautionary remark: The equa-
tion of Logos with masculine, and Eros with feminine cannot be
extended to mean men and women as specific, individual persons. Logos and Eros are fundamental principles of psychic life,
and both are active in members of both sexes.

[2]Neumann, *The Child*, p. 114.

In connection with the father archetype or Logos principle as the basis for social norms, however, it is interesting to note that gregarious animals (other than man) also have their social order. Their communities, too, need certain norms that are respected by all members of the group, in order to avoid constant fights among individuals which might endanger the survival of the species as a whole. Battles for rank in the pecking order are carried out to facilitate peaceful group life, with each individual animal knowing its place in the hierarchy and regulating its behavior accordingly. Of course, such social order in the animal kingdom is achieved not by conscious decision but rather through species-typical behavior patterns.

To a certain extent, however, animals do have their own equivalent of human morality, that is, behavior in keeping with certain socio-cultural norms. In a colony of jackdaws, for example, when two birds begin to fight, a third jackdaw of superior rank immediately intervenes. And the most interesting thing of all is that it invariably helps the weaker bird, in almost Christian fashion. In terms of animal behavior patterns, however, what happens is the following: Jackdaws are always more aggressive toward those birds closest to themselves in rank. So, when a superior jackdaw intervenes in a fight between two others, it automatically attacks the stronger, higher-ranking of the two fighting birds, thus indirectly protecting the weaker. Such "morality" is purposive, directed toward survival of the species, and serves to keep the group together.

This example was drawn from a book by the ethologist Wolfgang Wickler.[3] Along with Konrad Lorenz, I. Eibl-Eibesfeldt and others, Wickler is among those researchers who are using studies of comparative animal behavior to focus on those aspects of complex human behavior which are tribally preprogrammed. Wickler's book offers ample evidence to support his thesis that basic principles of moral behavior (e.g., the Ten Commandments) have their origins in biological constellations. Such evidence is of the greatest interest to exponents of Analytical Psychology, who are

---

[3]Wolfgang Wickler, *The Biology of the Ten Commandments*. New York: McGraw Hill, 1972, p. 66.

constantly concerned with the question of Man's "nature" in order to better recognize, by contrast, socio-cultural distortions and their neuroticizing effects on the individual—as self-estrangement from one's genuine humanity.

If it is true, as some behavioral researchers maintain, that the basic principles of morality have their origins in "biological constellations," this means nothing less than that they are archetypally inherent in "human nature." They are, in effect, psychic components archetypally active via the symbology of the paternal-masculine-spiritual. Among the animals these norms are built into the instinct system for the purpose of species and individual survival. The animal has no choice as to whether its behavior will conform to those guidelines. It is thus directly subject to a "spiritual" guidance within nature itself, which regulates animal behavior with purposive wisdom. It is for this reason that, in archaic human consciousness, the animal is often perceived as a divine creature, or at least as a channel through which the divine-spiritual manifests itself; the animal is, to a certain extent, closer to the spirit of Creation.

As a creature with ego-consciousness, "set free by nature" (in the words of H. Herder) and possessing freedom of decision, the human being must act in reaction or opposition to his own "instinctual nature." The predisposition to acquire such behavioral norms, however, is itself part of mankind's instinctual nature. It is an archetype whose dynamism takes visible form in the symbolism of the Paternal-Spiritual as expressed in such phenomena as the patriarchal deity of the Old Testament and His commandments. The archetypal forces of the Maternal and the Paternal, of Nature and Spirit, are in opposition to one another—and that opposition is an essential prerequisite for the development of a "freely deciding" consciousness. Thus it becomes clear that, in keeping with his specifically human "nature," Man must be characterized in essence as a creature of conflict.

The following observation is of special interest in this context: In the Old Testament, the patriarchal god Yahweh constantly insists upon his own uniqueness and omnipotence. At the same time, there is repeated reference to his jealousy of other gods, who are a constant temptation to his people. His worst enemy was Baal, who apparently exerted a seductive fascination, to the unfailing ire of the Old Testament prophets. Baal belonged to the circle of divinities around Astarte, the Great Mother Goddess; his cult was related to the fertility of nature and involved orgiastic rituals and temple prostitution.[4] All of this was abhorrent to Yahweh. Thus it might be said that, by means of his commandments, he fought against another mighty divinity, the Great Mother, as mankind's instinctual and "animal" nature. With the aid of the biblical commandments she was to be tamed, controlled and even repressed. Paternal and Maternal, Logos and Eros, constitute a pair of opposites, often in conflict. They are archetypal realities, generating constant tension in ego-consciousness. Freudian psychoanalysis speaks of the Ego serving as mediator between the instinctual Id and the limiting, ideal-generating Super-ego.

Mother Nature remains more or less the same in all times. She creates the fundamental bio-psychic needs and drives which serve the maintenance of life, its natural development and renewal. How human consciousness is to respond to and act toward this, its basic "nature," is transmitted by each society's system of guidelines and principles, the validity of which may be affirmed or denied to a certain extent. This is the realm of specifically human freedom.

Behavioral norms and guidelines are based on a particular *Weltanschauung*, the expression of a specific cultural canon and its value hierarchy. No matter how difficult it may be to break the taboos of one's own cultural canon in the face of social repression and inner feelings of guilt, this happens of necessity time and again. That is: In contrast to the bio-psychic, instinctual nature which is the realm of the Great Mother, world-views, values, principles and ethical imperatives change in the course of history and vary from culture to culture. These days they are often examined purely from a sociological viewpoint and regarded as exclusively socially determined.

But the vital need for principles of order, and the creativity to develop them, strongly indicate that they are an archetypal component of human nature and thus are consonant with a fundamental, instinctual pattern. Behavioral norms are evidently linked to

[4]V. Maag, "Syrien—Palästina" (Syria—Palestine), in Schmökel, *Kulturgeschichte des alten Orients* (Cultural History of the Ancient Orient). Stuttgart: Kroner, 1961, pp. 595 ff.

mankind's gift of consciousness and have an archetypal base, regardless of the specific content of such guidelines and the degree to which that content may change historically.

The father archetype, like all others, is not symbolized only in personified form. Its attendant Logos principle, for example, is often graphically represented by the image of the sword, which symbolizes active confrontation, separation, decision, differentiation, as well as being associated with masculine sexuality.[5]

At the same time, the sword is an instrument of death. Inimical elements are separated out,[6] which in psychological terms brings up associations to "defense mechanisms" such as repression, denial, etc. Thus the totality of nature's effects is fragmented, sectioned, divided up. Opposites are keenly recognized and analyzed, which can be carried to extremes of hairsplitting sophistry, in which razor-sharp mental agility is exercised.

Another graphic symbol of Logos is the wind. In the Greek language the word *anemos* means both "wind" and "spirit." (The Latin *animus*, on the other hand, is used only in the extended sense.) Wind is invisible of itself, but has a powerful potential effectiveness. It can stir up dust, whip up water. We can clearly feel the strength and effects of the wind, but we can never see it itself. It is the diametric opposite of plastic, tangible or vivid. There is, then, an obvious parallel to all that we generally regard as belonging to the "spiritual" or "intellectual" realms.

In the ancient Babylonian creation myth *Enuma Elish,* which tells of the struggle of the cosmic gods against their mother Thiamat, the dragon of Chaos, the hero Marduk mobilizes the four winds to surround Chaos on all sides and thus localize it/her. This enables Marduk to capture the dragon in his net, after which it/she is cut into pieces with the sword, giving rise to the various parts of the world, mountains, rivers, etc.

This is a splendidly graphic illustration of how Logos strives to localize and capture—i.e., to conceptualize—all that is chaotic, unformed and hence dangerous. The next step in the process is dif-

---

[5]In the German text, the author here makes use of the multiple applications of the root word *scheid*, which is an element in numerous verbs and nouns dealing with separation, decision and differentiation, as well as the word *Scheide*, which means both "sheath" and "vagina."—*Trans*.

[6]*Ausgeschieden*, again using the root "scheid."—*Trans*.

ferentiation. Out of all this comes Cosmos, the Greek word for order, which also serves as a symbol for the realm of consciousness and its capacity for orientation. Creation myths are at the same time myths of the dawn of human consciousness, since to our perception the world exists only to the extent that we are conscious of it.

The father archetype, too, can manifest itself in constructive, life-promoting ways and in destructive and terrible forms. On the one hand it stimulates the process of intellectual confrontation; as *Logos spermatikos* (the seed-bearing spirit) it engenders consciousness and stands for the possibility of a differentiated orientation to the world by means of categories and norms. But as the sky-god Uranos, who tries to confine his children in the bowels of Mother Earth (i.e., is "repressive" in the true sense of the word), he is opposed to any form of renewal and thus is in effect anti-life. The same applies to his successor Kronos, who swallowed his own children.

Here we have a mythic image of that conservative patriarchal consciousness which insists on a position once it has been taken and will use any and all means to deter and repress psychic or social renewal. Such a spirit has manifested itself repeatedly in the course of human history. It is frequently encountered in the individual realm as well, often responsible for neuroses based upon a blockage of the processes of psychic life. In folklore and fairytales the destructive masculine spirit is typified by characters of the Bluebeard type, who mangle, dismember and kill feminine life, and by the troll or mountain spirit who so totally binds the Princess by his magical omniscience that she is rendered incapable of undertaking any life-oriented relationships.[7]

[7]See Mario Jacoby, V. Kast, and I. Riedel, *Das Böse im Märchen* (Evil in Fairytales). Fellbach: Bonz, 1978.

11. Maternal Behavior and Women's Liberation

We now enter the realm characterized by Neumann when he referred to "the intervention of the patriarchal principle of order represented by the mother's consciousness and her animi."[1] Jung used the term *animus* to designate the effects of the masculine Logos principle in the psychic life of woman.[2] He did not mean by this the capacity for rational thought and differentiation available to a woman's ego-consciousness, which develops in the course of experience and is flexible enough to adapt to changing situations. Rather, in using the term animus Jung tried to give an appropriate name to an autonomous Logos principle operating out of a woman's unconscious. This autonomous, unconscious Logos may manifest itself in a creative spiritual or intellectual quality, or in bold initiative and energy. But it may also show itself in an overly critical attitude toward one's surroundings and a compulsive need to indulge in destructive self-criticism.

It is this latter, negative animus quality that is graphically symbolized in the femininity-destroying figure of Bluebeard. As a personality develops, the potency of this Logos-animus is enriched by contents (attitudes, judgments) internalized from parents and from the entire socio-cultural value system. Thus the animus may also manifest itself in second-hand opinions which seem so convincing that their validity is never even questioned. In the thera-

[1] *The Child*, p. 114.
[2] See Emma Jung, *Animus and Anima*. New York: The Analytical Psychology Club of New York, 1957.

peutic analysis of such animus manifestations it usually becomes evident that there is strong resistance to the examination of these emotionally toned opinions—as if some sort of heresy were involved in calling sacrosanct matters into question. The process generates the kind of anxiety usually related to the breaking of serious taboos.

Animus problems constitute a broad and complex field, for the further illumination of which readers are advised to consult the relevant literature.[3]

The patriarchal repression of women, so decried today, was possible in the first place largely because many forms of the "patriarchal principle of order" were accepted as valid by women themselves. In its aspect as an internalized cultural canon, the animus was thus identical with the collective principle of order and its values.

In our brief excursion into ethnology we saw that maternal behavior toward infants can vary considerably from culture to culture. Within each society, the "proper" way to provide mothering appears to be culturally prescribed and accepted by that society's mothers. It is impossible to determine with absolute certainty to what extent such maternal behavior is species-appropriate, i.e., in keeping with the mother archetype, and to what extent it is modified (positively or negatively) by the patriarchal principle of order linked to the father archetype. The reason such a determination is impossible is because every analysis of the situation is in turn colored by the Logos of the observer and the influence of the current *Zeitgeist*.

But this much can be said with some degree of certainty: In their role behavior, mothers follow the dictates of a tribal (or national, or class) cultural canon which they inwardly perceive as offering valid and true guidelines. Throughout much of Western history women apparently have identified themselves unquestioningly with the place assigned to them in a "God-given" social order. The documentation offered by L. de Mause[4] makes an impressive case for the view that the *Zeitgeist* which manifested itself

[3]See ibid. and also C. G. Jung, *Collected Works*, Vols. 7 and 11.
[4]*Hört ihr die Kinder weinen* (Hear the Children Crying), pp. 55–58.

during a good deal of that history was seriously disruptive of what Neumann would have seen as species-appropriate maternal behavior.

Since the advent of the Industrial Revolution a change has taken place in the history of the human spirit. The realization that machinery and the expanding potential of technology are enabling humanity to increasingly control its own fate has created a faith in progress and in the realizability of human happiness. Parallel to this has come a growing secularization and the calling into question of all "divinely ordained" social, religious and cultural value systems. Nietzsche wrote of the transvaluation of all values.

The content of today's "patriarchal principle of order" is thus difficult to define. It appears to be threatened by the chaos of dissolution. The decay of widely accepted values is often seen as the crisis of our times. But though it indeed brings crisis, the decay of a reigning system of values also compels the search for new meaning and new attitudes. The catalogue of problems facing the world today is vast; it hardly needs discussion here. But it is also frequently pointed out with pride that broad segments of the world's population are now undergoing a modern, historically revolutionary and extremely valuable expansion of consciousness.

In the work referred to earlier, for example, L. de Mause[5] sings the praises of what he terms the "supportive" system of child-rearing, which takes empathic account of a child's needs while avoiding too many parental projections. In his view, such a child-rearing system calls for a degree of emotional maturity on the part of parents which was not widely available prior to the middle of this century.

If such progress is indeed being made, it is certainly due in part to the insights provided by modern depth psychology. The research of Freud, Adler and Jung yielded an understanding of psychic processes which, though perhaps previously adumbrated by a few literary, philosophical or religious geniuses, had not been available before to the general public or even to the uses of psychotherapy.

[5]Ibid.

It might also be said that the *Zeitgeist* in today's Western industrial societies places a high value on the concept of emancipation. The ideas of fairness and equality of opportunity for individual liberation—even despite unfavorable social and material conditions—are decidedly modern, particularly with respect to the very serious efforts to translate those ideas into reality. But since it is primarily the state that is in a position to effect such a translation, we find ourselves in the paradoxical situation of emphasizing collective and individual emancipation while at the same time developing an increasingly state-dominated society—yet another seemingly insoluble problem on our lengthy list.

Emancipation is not possible without the dissolution of existing values. A patriarchal system of order compels its members to unquestioning and unhesitating adoption of its value hierarchy. The Latin verb *emancipare*, however, originally meant "to release a grown son or a slave from patriarchal care into independence." In an extended sense, emancipation later also came to mean the liberation from inner chains which have been imposed through widely accepted attitudes, prejudices, and traditions.

As we all know, efforts at the emancipation of women began at the end of the last century, with an attempt to break out of the role of being "only a woman" (with all its attendant limitations on active participation in social and public life) and to achieve equality with men. In psychological terms, the "Logos animus" of a few women began to creatively criticize prevalent conditions —or, in other terms still, identification with the existing patriarchal value system began to crumble.

The danger of such basically important, progressive and creative ideas is that they may easily be overvalued and result in fanatical, obsessive behavior. At the same time it may be that, in the realms of culture and *Weltanschauung*, a revolutionary new order cannot be established without people who are obsessed by new ideas. The obsession provides the necessary impetus to insure that a "new wind" not only blows but penetrates and is widely felt. In their fanatical enthusiasm, however, the early suffragettes were unconscious of the fact that they themselves had fallen into the trap of valuing the masculine above the feminine, that they were devaluing and rejecting the realm of the mother

archetype by trying to be just like men. Nevertheless, an important start was made at that time.

According to both official statistics and individual studies,[6] in
recent decades increasing numbers of women—and especially
mothers—have been integrated into the labor force. Modern industrial societies can no longer do without the collaboration of
both single and married women. In other words, women today
need no longer feel themselves tied to home and hearth; their role
is no longer clearly prescribed. Of course, women worked in archaic societies as well. The big difference is that in more primitive
societies there was (and is) not such a rigorous separation between
home and workplace. Mothers in archaic societies usually carried
their infants along with them when they worked. Today's separation of home and workplace creates a host of new problems, oc-
casioned by the frequent loss of the intimate relationship to the
mother during early infancy.

A patriarchal system of order which confines woman to roles
as childbearer, cook and housekeeper would by and large violate
the tenets of today's collective consciousness, which is much less
rigid in its views on woman's place in the overall scheme of
things. The patriarchal principle of order now finds itself in the
midst of a crisis of values. The kind of fate which befell Nora in
Ibsen's famous play *A Doll's House* would be something of a rarity
in the modern West today. But the process is not yet complete.
There is still some way to go before full equality will be achieved,
including equal job opportunity for women, equal pay for equal
work, and true equality before the law.

From the psychological standpoint there is another problem.
Each liberation from an existing value system also creates insecu-
rity and disorientation. In our own time, medical, psychological
and pedagogical knowledge as well as practical assistance with
child-rearing are more urgently needed than ever. There is a
widespread faith in science, coupled with the hope that it will provide the orientation needed for the optimal raising of children.
As a depth psychologist, one should really approve of this
development, since it may help to generate a more genuine rela-

[6]See, for example, E. Koliadis, *Mütterliche Erwerbstätigkeit und kindliche
Sozialisation* (Working Mothers and the Socialization of Children). Weinheim
& Basel: Beltz, 1975.

tionship to children and to eliminate some prejudices and unfounded opinions.

But faith in medical science and the popularization of psychological theories create yet another difficulty. The various sciences devoted to the study of mankind are not in agreement on many points and thus issue conflicting practical recommendations. For example: Physicians often suggest that infants be permitted to cry and be nursed only at regular intervals, since this strengthens the lungs and accustoms the child to a rhythmic pattern which is also good for the digestive system; giving the child a pacifier or letting it suck its thumb is rejected because of later damage to teeth and jaw structure.[7] But most students of depth psychology would propose exactly the opposite. It would appear, then, that science can provide whichever arguments happen to suit one's own predilections.

Moreover, while the concepts of depth psychology are based on direct experience of the psyche, as "ideas" they are somewhat abstracted from experience and interwoven with more or less speculative, explanatory hypotheses. Hence it cannot be assumed that the general public will properly grasp the significance of publications in that field. Further: All that depth psychology can more or less convincingly do is to set up hypotheses about the "laws" of psychic processes on the basis of what is average or usual. The most vital aspect of that ultimately mysterious creature Man, however, consists in an infinite number of individual variables. Statements by writers in the field of depth psychology must therefore be integrated by readers into their own range of personal experience.

Books on psychology are attempts at clarifying the nature and workings of the human psyche. But unless they function as catalysts, providing terms and formulations for subliminal feelings and perceptions, they fail to carry out their true purpose. The term "Aha reaction" is a succinct formula meant to describe such a process. But a reader's "Aha reaction" can also be generated by "creative misunderstandings," in which his or her own preconceptions are projected into a writer's statements even when there is very little congruence between them. Often enough, the ideas

[7]F. Renggli, *Angst und Geborgenheit* (Fear and Security), pp. 246–247.

of depth psychology remain over-intellectualized concepts which are not integrated into subjective individual experience and thus lead only to schematic comprehension. For this reason, psychology books cannot be expected to provide much help in dealing with an individual's unique constellation of problems.

But despite all this uncertainty, experience has shown that archetypal levels of experience exert their influence on the psyche of every mother. The conflict and interplay of mother and father archetypes, of Eros and Logos, are manifested in endless personal variations. Despite the dissolution of a generally accepted patriarchal principle of order, the attitude of each individual mother to her child and to her own maternity is influenced by the value systems of her social class, family tradition and perhaps some enlightened "science." Women today, however, are increasingly caught in a conflict between their maternal role and their legitimate need for self-realization.

Some degree of psychological understanding of the primal relationship and its disturbances has become quite widespread in our own time. Most mothers are now aware of how important empathic, loving care during infancy can be for a child's later development. According to Neumann, a successful primal relationship is greatly facilitated when the partriarchal principle of order, manifesting itself through the Logos animus, is integrated into the matriarchal constellation of the primal relationship. Such a situation is portrayed in those myths where the Great Mother Goddess dominates, with masculine figures ranged alongside or, more frequently, in subordinate positions.[8]

Psychologically speaking, in this phase the critical-evaluating Logos attitudes should serve the matriarchal principle. This means, in effect, an attitude which regards the facts and experiences of motherhood and the dual union as the supreme value, and is subservient to it. To a Logos-animus with such an orientation, living in intimate and empathic relationship to the needs of a child would not be derided as merely "the life of a brood mare" or perceived as violating the "higher" aspects of a woman's personality.

But this would appear to be an idealized image of mother-love and maternal happiness. And like every ideal, it calls for a certain

[8]*The Child*, pp. 98–99.

degree of skepticism. Real human behavior can be perfectly harmonized with an ideal only by dint of repression or suppression of those tendencies which run counter to it. Even through identification with an ideal image, such contrary tendencies, though pushed aside, cannot be entirely eliminated—certainly not from the inner world of the psyche. (This is a basic fact of psychic life the knowledge of which we owe primarily to Freud's work.) The suppressed or repressed contents will make themselves felt, unbidden, often unconsciously, generally in some inappropriate form. And they will inevitably have their effect on a mother's behavior toward her child.

In the work cited earlier, F. Renggli[9] graphically describes maternal behavior among the South Seas tribe of the Ifaluk, where "the child is king" and there is a generally accepted obligation to give special love and affirmation to every child. Women are valued more highly than men among these people, because they can bear children. At the same time, infants are subjected to such painful procedures as cold and hot shocks and a kind of water feeding that often results in asphyxiation. When a child treated in this way begins to scream loudly enough, it is pacified with the mother's breast. It is as if the benevolent maternal heart must be repeatedly jolted awake by actively torturing or passively watching the torment of the infant.

In our latitudes, too, self-sacrificing mother-love is generally accompanied by unconscious resentment. Even when, out of whatever motives, a mother fully identifies with her child's needs and is always there for it in the positive sense from the infant's standpoint, a tribute is often exacted at a later time; the child may become so much a part of the mother's sense of herself that she is later unable to set it free for the sake of its own independent development, and thus becomes a possessive mother.

Rightly understood, however, the idea of woman's emancipation as a striving for self-realization is psychically vital. It generally cannot be repressed with impunity, since a woman's Logos-animus pushes for its realization in some appropriate form and puts up serious resistance against complete identification with the maternal role. Many women today are constitutionally unable to accept being "only a mother" even for a limited period of a few

[9]*Angst und Geborgenheit* (Fear and Security).

years. Doing so would constitute an inner violation, which would be beneficial neither to their own emotional balance nor to their impact upon their children. (Aside from a woman's own inner factors, of course, maternal behavior must also be viewed in the light of a specific marital situation.)

The conflict between the maternal role and the need for self-realization is often a grave one these days. In the deepest sense the entire complex of experiences revolving around motherhood and child-rearing is certainly an important component of a woman's individuation. But this does not preclude conflict; on the contrary, it includes it, and the question of how it can be resolved is a recurring one.

We have seen how kibbutz mothers are relieved of many maternal duties by having child care organized collectively. Feminist literature also often suggests that it would be better to have children cared for collectively by trained personnel. The assumption is that, thus relieved of much of their constricting burden, mothers would take greater joy in their children and devote to them a more genuine concern. On this subject the feminist author Jutta Menschik has written:

> It is noteworthy that prominent feminists have thus far not come up with constructive proposals for the vital conflict of "mother-child-career." Yet precisely this conflict, which is often relegated to the individual level, must be elevated to a social plane, in the sense that societal solutions are formulated and carried out.[10]

Somehow, something certainly must be done to ease the extreme time- and energy-consuming burdens of child care for those mothers who cannot get along without a broader personal or professional field of activity.

[10]J. Menschik, *Feminismus* (Feminism). Cologne: Pahl-Rugenstein, 1977, p. 183.

12. Motherhood and Career

In view of the psychological importance of the "primary other" in a child's development, the question of whether the mothers of small children should undertake to work outside the home is the subject of heated discussion and extreme generalization in the public at large and among researchers. E. Koliadis has published a monograph on "Working Mothers and the Socialization of Children"[1] based on an analysis of empirical investigations. Its chief conclusions are as follows:

Working mothers who perceive their jobs as satisfying have a positive and "warmhearted" relationship to their children. Such mothers use milder disciplinary measures and their style of child-rearing is more tolerant, characterized by consistency and relatedness to the child. Mothers who are dissatisfied with their jobs—a situation which is determined to a great extent by the kind of work involved—demonstrate less positive emotional relations with their children, who tend to be overburdened with household chores. The child-rearing practices of such mothers are predominantly characterized by inconsistency and uncertainty.

The most severely limited in their child-rearing attitudes, however, turned out to be those non-working mothers who were dissatisfied with their role as housewife (women who wanted to work but refrained from doing so out of a "sense of duty"). They had less trusting and feelingful relations to their children and less sureness in their own maternal and pedagogical qualities.[2]

[1]*Mütterliche Erwerbstätigkeit und kindliche Sozialisation* (Working Mothers and the Socialization of Children).
[2]Ibid., p. 339.

97

This is followed by another important point:

> The greater and stronger the father's participation and engagement in family problems and household tasks, the more positive his attitude toward his wife's work, and the more his view of their respective roles is that of partnership, the more does the wife tend to be satisfied with her outside work and the more easily do the children accept the fact that their mother works.[3]
>
> In general it can be said that the fact of a mother's working constitutes a factor hindering socialization only if a family's emotional climate is disturbed, if tensions, conflict situations and pathogenic factors predominate and the children (especially very young ones) are left without adequate substitute care during the mother's working time away from home.[4]

And a final quote:

> Our analysis of the literature has also shown that even the fact of a mother's not working can become a pedagogical problem if her overprotectiveness, so common in the modern nuclear family, forces the children into a certain substitute role in which they are supposed to assist the parents (especially the mother) in dealing with their own conflicts.[5]

These conclusions speak for themselves and need no further interpretation. Having been derived from empirical research based largely on statistics, they too deal with a kind of "average" of interdependence between maternal behavior and child socialization, and therefore may not always apply to an individual situation. Properly understood, however, the general guidelines they contain can indeed be of help to individual mothers. One of the most sympathetic and reality-oriented things about the Koliadis monograph is that it closes with the following quote from the writings of U. Lehr:

> "It would be both impossible and irresponsible to try and set up a list of generally optimal conditions for socialization! What must never be forgotten is the vast number of intervening variables, whose varying importance and specific interaction in a given situation, coupled with the personality of the child-rearer

[3]Ibid., p. 340.
[4]Ibid., p. 344.
[5]Ibid.

and that of the child, can result in extremely divergent kinds and degrees of socialization even under externally comparable conditions . . . But since no generally valid catalogue of child-rearing behavior can be set up to apply to varying family situations, there is a constant need for individual diagnosis and counseling which aims at taking account of the interplay of variables in a given situation."[6]

Individual counseling is also the task of the psychotherapist who bases his work on depth psychology. It is my experience that a great many mothers today suffer from strong feelings of ambivalence toward their infants and young children. Often what is behind these feelings is the conflict we have already discussed between an understanding of the need for a successful primal relationship and a woman's legitimate need for a broader framework for her own self-realization. This tension sometimes develops into a severe conflict of conscience, which can go so far that mothers are plagued by what they experience as a compulsion to kill their children, in turn resulting in severe feelings of guilt and anxiety.

Closer analysis generally reveals that these mothers are suffering the after-effects of a disturbed primal relationship in their own infancy. On the conscious level, these women are eager to do a good mothering job, since they know from first-hand experience what it means for a child to be faced by a withholding or unsympathetic parent. But in some cases the effect of a disturbed primal relationship experienced in the mother's own childhood takes the form of strong identification with the Logos-animus, so that the conflict is experienced in an especially intense manner. The important thing in most of these cases is to avoid taking a morally superior position, since that can only heighten a woman's guilt feelings about being a "bad mother."

In addition to the analysis of its personal implications, this conflict must also be taken seriously as a problem of our times. It does not arise only because of factors in a person's individual history and cannot be cleared up by means of therapeutic analysis alone. It is an integral part of the real and widespread problems facing

[6]U. Lehr, *Die Bedeutung der Familie im Sozialisationsprozess* (The Importance of the Family in the Socialization Process). Stuttgart: Kohlhammer, 1973, p. 87, quoted in E. Koliadis, *Mütterliche Erwerbstätigkeit und kindliche Sozialisation* (Working Mothers and the Socialization of Children), p. 346.

our society today. Despite all idealization of a successful primal relationship and of genuine mother-love, I regard it as important that this problem facing so many modern women be taken seriously, so that they do not guiltily misapprehend themselves as inadequate mothers.

It is very difficult to resolve this conflict. For many women the harmonizing of the double role is an almost unbearable burden. In most cases, moreover, it is further complicated by yet a third factor—the need to be a genuine partner in the marriage relationship. Given the existing circumstances in our society, solutions such as those tried on the Israeli kibbutz or in various modern communes are neither likely to work nor, in the final analysis, particularly desirable for a majority of mothers. In any case, they would call for significant changes in the society as a whole.

The idea that a way could be found to achieve a problem-free harmonization of women's conflicting needs and the requirements of an optimal primal relationship for their children is certainly linked to "expectations of Paradise." The longing for an unconflicted, paradisial existence often takes on a regressive character and in some circumstances is projected onto "society," which is then expected to serve as the benevolent, conflict-resolving "environment mother." On the other hand—and this will be dealt with in greater detail later—even though ideas of a better existence may be mixed with elements of utopian perfection and bliss, they may provide the stimulus for creative attempts at problem-solving. Without the specifically human idea that things could be other (and better) than they are, there would be no movement at all.

But, as the English writer Jerome K. Jerome so aptly put it: "In this world, I've noticed, very few things come up to the image we have of them." Whatever his sympathies, an analytical psychologist finds it difficult to identify completely with programs aimed at a broad general resolution of society's problems. This is due to the realization that no projected solution can ever do justice to the complexity of the human psyche and thus must always be burdened with shadow aspects as "the other side of the coin."

No general solution will prove ideal to the problems facing today's mothers. In many instances what is needed is simply perseverance, bearing up and working through the suffering, with here and there the possibility of relief through flexible, individually tailored measures. Suffering and dealing with conflicts is, after all, the basic material out of which human maturation is forged. Although this may not enable a mother to provide ideal maternal care, her own maturing should help her to develop empathic reactions to her child by giving her direct insight into the pain, the highs and lows, in the life of the soul, and thus a genuine understanding for the child's inherent development potential as well as its recurring crises.

These observations bring to a close our excursion into the inexhaustible theme of mother-child relations. It would seem to have led us far afield from our immediate subject, the concept of Paradise. But in reality we have never lost sight of it, for we have been speaking of conflicts that are inherent in the human psyche—ones that also play a role in maternal behavior. In biblical language this is expressed as: "And I will put enmity between thee (the serpent) and the woman, and between thy seed and her seed." Another relevant biblical passage is: "In the sweat of thy face shalt thou eat bread . . ." which refers to the necessity for human labor, giving rise to a broad range of social implications—including the questions of women's liberation we have touched upon.

Our observations have thus, unremarked, moved us closer to Judeo-Christian concepts of a lost Paradise. At this point it would seem appropriate to examine the biblical text (Genesis 2:5–3:24) for its psychological significance.

PART TWO

A PSYCHOLOGICAL INTERPRETATION OF THE BIBLICAL TALE OF PARADISE AND THE FALL

1. An Analysand's Fantasy of Paradise

A 22-year-old man began analysis with me complaining that life struck him as absurd, simply Kafkaesque, as he preferred to call it. It was this feeling of life's absurdity, coupled with recurring stomach cramps, that had prompted him to overcome his grave reservations and attempt analysis.

In his initial dream he lived in a strangely complex residence which had only small, high slit-windows and many incomprehensible, senseless rules about how the curtains were to be drawn. The dreamer rebelled against those rules.

The theme of rebellion, of furious resentment against the conditions of his existence, occupied the foreground of this man's waking reality as well. In order not to be isolated in his anger, which came to be directed against the "establishment" and society as a whole, he joined a leftist political group. But even there, he soon felt that he could not find the sense of sharing for which he longed. Disillusioned by the power struggles, intrigues and naiveté he found in this group, he soon withdrew. Once again, he felt, he had not been truly understood.

What did he want out of life? In the course of analysis the following fantasies were brought to light, directly or indirectly: He wanted to live in the country, in a beautiful natural setting, far from traffic noise, frenzy, polluted air, in a house of his own. Of course, he did not want to live alone, but with the woman who would be his "predestined partner," as he often put it. It would be this woman who would make possible his full development, not only as a person but as an artist. (He was, in fact, a very gifted painter.)

His entire relation to the female sex showed how important it was to him that his predestined partner be someone formed out of his own rib, flesh of his flesh. The partly unconscious image which he nurtured bore the following characteristics:

His partner would mother him, carrying him protectively in her arms, so to speak; but she would also have to be capable of letting him go whenever he needed it, or else he would feel himself imprisoned and forced to break out. She would inspire him, be independent in thought and feeling, yet not so much so that he would be made insecure or envious by her superiority. Her tender understanding would free him from suffering, frustration and a sense of inferiority. But she must also be open to the many things he had to give her; his own happiness required that he see himself as a generous bestower of gifts rather than just childishly dependent. In short, along with everything else the woman would have to admire him.

Such expectations were constantly disappointed, of course, which often sent him into a fury. He railed against the social order which violated his personhood, against his own fate and, as someone who had had a strict Catholic upbringing, against God as well. Above all, this young man refused to accept the fact of death, retreating into gloom whenever his dreams dealt with gravestones or dead people who had been run over.

When I remarked that he apparently longed for a paradisial sense of existence free of all tension and disturbance, and that although he knew better he repeatedly tried to force life into that mold, my analysand replied that indeed this was precisely what he wanted—in fact, he felt it was owed to him.

Some time later, however, he had the following dream: "I wander through a gloomy church or castle, weary as always. Then I hear a loud voice announcing that I may enter Paradise. A large iron door opens, behind which I see green fields, trees and many peaceable animals. But when I get to the door I say that I do not want to enter Paradise yet."

Here are some salient facts from this young man's background: During her pregnancy his mother had suffered from pyelitis. and our patient was reportedly born two months prematurely. He remembered his mother, moreover, as an extremely insecure and anxious person. At the age of nine he developed the idea that she wanted to poison him, as a result of which he was sent to a child psychologist (a woman) for treatment. Clearly what is at work here is a disturbance of the *Urbeziehung*, of the primal relationship, as described by Erich Neumann.

I have presented this case from my own practice because it involves a personal fantasy of Paradise which closely approximates the archetypal form described in Genesis. For this analysand the fantasy had evolved into an emotionally charged, dominant idea linked to a longing for security in the infant's "unitary reality." As we have already remarked, when the primal relationship is disturbed, the sense of safety and containment which is natural to the unitary reality of a child's first year is seriously shaken by menacing, anxiety-producing failures of parental caring. Paradise may then be transformed into Hell. Serious developmental disturbances are the result. I have observed in such cases that quite often an unquenched thirst for paradisial security may linger into adult life, coupled with an inability to bear conflict and suffering or to work them through meaningfully.

This was my patient's problem. After his dream I asked him why he had not left the gloomy church and entered such an inviting Paradise. He replied that he had somehow gotten an eerie feeling: In his dream he had vaguely thought that entering Paradise would mean his death, so he had elected to remain in the dim church, "weary as always." Through this dream he first became conscious that his yearnings for Paradise involved life-denying regression.

A year later this analysand had the following dream: "I am with someone, and we have moved. We inhabit two or three derelict houses. Two of them are so exposed to traffic noise that I go in search of our house by the lake. It has no walls and its board floors lead directly out into the water. Nevertheless it is here that I want to stay. Only here can I find the peace I need in order to work."

Without attempting any detailed interpretation of this dream, I should like to point out that it represents the first time that the dreamer chooses to remain in a residence *despite* its shortcomings. During that same period, in his waking life he was able for the first time to establish a deep relationship with a woman despite the fact that all was not perfect harmony. This time, he tried to work out conflicts with his partner. In other words there was a gradual relinquishing of his demand for paradisial bliss, a tentative start at learning to deal with the "shadow" in himself and in the world around him, without excessive panic. That was an important developmental step, achieved through the therapy.

It must be admitted that my analysand's fantasies of Paradise are very attractive. The return to nature; relief from noise, air pollution and urban blight; release from the compulsion to achieve—all of these would be desirable. But when there is a disturbance of the primal relationship, adaptation to what is termed "reality" cannot be experienced as desirable or meaningful. Life's reality is instead perceived as the devouring or castrating environment mother. Images of paradisial security then come to dominate the overall psychic economy.

2. The Creation of Eve from Adam's Rib

My analysand's wishful thinking about a "predestined partner" prompted me to attempt an interpretation of the famous and infamous biblical passage describing the creation of Eve from Adam's rib (Genesis 2:21–22). As "bone of my bones, flesh of my flesh," the woman in my patient's fantasy was what current psychoanalytic terminology calls a narcissistic object.[1] His predestined partner was to have her own subjectivity and *Lebensraum* only to the extent that this would not disrupt his fantasy of total unity or collide with his symbiotic needs. She was to be, in brief, part of *his* private world-design; her own independent existence was not to inject any conflict into the unitary reality for which he yearned.

From the standpoint of Jungian psychology, the phenomenon we have been describing is a projection of the anima. There is an old saying that every man carries his own Eve inside him. This expresses very succinctly an important aspect of Jung's ideas about the anima as the feminine soul-image in a man's psyche.[2] As long as a real woman serves exclusively as the carrier of a man's anima-projection, she is experienced by him unconsciously as nothing but a narcissistic object. Only the withdrawal of that projection would give the woman sufficient space to manifest her own personality and at the same time give the man some insight

[1]See, for example, the chapter on Alter-Ego (pp. 140ff.) in H. Kohut, *The Analysis of Self*. New York: International University Press, 1971.
[2]See, for example, C. G. Jung, *Collected Works*, Vol. 7, pp. 188ff., and Vol. 9, II, pp. 20ff.; also Emma Jung, *Animus and Anima*.

into the nature of his own anima fantasies and their attendant expectations, longings and emotions.

But the withdrawal of projection is itself an act of increased consciousness which dissolves the paradisial unitary reality. It means that the differentness of both partners in a relationship, and the discrepancies in their respective needs, must be emotionally recognized and acknowledged, which of necessity leads to conflict situations.

There is a question, of course, as to whether a psychological interpretation of Genesis 2:21–22 as describing a "narcissistic object relationship" is legitimate. This biblical passage has been used countless times to justify the view that women are inferior to men. Since Eve was created from Adam's rib, she was the *second* human to be created, and this has been taken to indicate her secondary rank.[3] In the First Letter of Paul to Timothy the following passage appears: "Let a woman learn in silence with all submissiveness. I permit no woman to teach or to have authority over men; she is to keep silent. For Adam was formed first, then Eve" (I Timothy 2:11–13).

At the Council of Mâcon in the year 585 the question was raised as to whether a woman had a soul, and even in the 17th century men were not quite sure "whether women be human beings. . . ."[4] The inferiority and badness ascribed to women was given its worst form in the *Malleus Maleficarum* written in 1487 by two Dominican monks with the blessing of Pope Innocent VIII, a document which, as has already been mentioned, served as the foundation for the witchhunts of the Inquisition. There it was stated: "Since women are faulty in all the powers of the soul and the body, it be in no way astonishing that they cause all manner of iniquitous deeds to be done against those with whom they are in rivalry . . . These faults are also distinguishable by the manner of creation of the first woman, in that she was formed from a crooked rib."[5]

[3]Jolande Jacobi, *Complex, Archetype, Symbol*. Bollingen Series LVII. New York: Pantheon Books, 1959, p. 18.
[4]From a 1617 document cited in ibid., p. 18.
[5]J. Sprenger and H. Institoris, *Der Hexenhammer* (The "Malleus Maleficorum"), Vol. 1. Berlin: Barsdorf Verlag, 1906, pp. 97ff.

In any case, this biblical passage has been used repeatedly to buttress man's claim to dominance over woman. Certainly the Yahwist scribe injected the patriarchal self-image and world-view of Israelite culture into his creation tale. K. A. Bruning, a prehistorian, points out that when the story of the Fall was composed, woman had already been forced from the highly respected position she had once enjoyed in the ancient Orient.[6]

An unequivocally patriarchal tone is clearly evident in Genesis 3:16: " . . . your desire shall be for your husband, and he shall rule over you." This statement appears to be part of the theological-heuristic side of the Yahwist story. But the mythical image of the creation of woman did not necessarily arise out of patriarchal prejudice. A. Rosenberg suggests that the verse "Therefore a man leaves his father and his mother and cleaves to his wife" (Genesis 2:24) points in quite another direction: "This is a social aspect which would have been impossible in a patriarchal society; for within such a system the man brings the woman home to his paternal clan."[7]

From the psychological standpoint, perhaps an appropriate interpretation would be that in a creation myth—which is always at the same time an account of the dawn of consciousness—a unity must inevitably evolve into a pair of opposites. If this were not to happen, that which was created would rest in its unity and the process of life would come to a standstill. The development of consciousness always presupposes the opposition of subject and object. From the first man (who in some mythologies is portrayed as bisexual, a hermaphrodite) there thus develop the "opposites" of man and woman. From the unity of one there comes at first two-in-unity, until the "Fall" creates polarity. The true coming-to-consciousness takes place only at the Tree of Knowledge. From that point onward mankind must live out the consequences of the knowledge that Adam and Eve are not only one

[6]K. A. Bruning, "Die Sache mit Eva—in der Sicht des Vorgeschichtlers" (The Business with Eve—from the Perspective of the Prehistorian), in *Die Sache mit dem Apfel* (The Business with the Apple), by J. Illies. Freiburg im Breisgau: Herder, 1972, pp. 34–35.

[7]A. Rosenberg, "Das älteste Drama" (The Oldest Drama), in *Die Sache mit dem Apfel* (The Business with the Apple), by J. Illies, p. 69.

flesh but in many respects diametrically different. It is at this point that the Yahwist scribe expresses the theology appropriate to his time, particularly in ascribing the different punishments and life-tasks to man and woman.

It is in keeping with psychological experience that the longing for Paradise, for unitary reality, often includes the yearning for a predestined partner who, as a narcissistic object, is always there for the purpose of serving one's own needs. In other words, the regressive form of the mother complex becomes acute, and it becomes difficult to affirm the conflicts and demands of reality.

3. On Textual Criticism of the Biblical Tale of Paradise (Genesis 2:5–3:24)

At this point, for the sake of completeness, we shall briefly examine the current state of Old Testament research as it applies to the tale of Paradise.

Aside from a few features, biblical scholars today feel that the story of Paradise and the Fall is not indigenous Israelite material; it is thought that, in all probability, the Israelites acquired the idea of Paradise from Canaanite culture. Especially such images as the heavenly mountain and the divine garden, the tree of life and the water of life, cherubim and the divine flame of lightning, as well as the image of a primal man without flaw or sin—all of these are now thought to have their origins in the imagery common to the ancient Middle East.[1]

It should be mentioned here that critical biblical research began during the last century to subject the so-called historical books of the Bible to systematic analysis with regard to their vocabulary, grammatical structures, style and conceptual content. The countless "doublettes"—two, sometimes even three slightly varied reports of one and the same event—attracted the attention of researchers. It soon became clear that the biblical Scriptures could not have come from a single source and a single author, but had been assembled and woven together from many sources. The various Scriptures were the expression of various historical and

[1]H. Haag, *Der Mensch am Anfang* (Mankind at the Beginning). Trier: Paulinus Verlag, 1970, p. 3.

religious views, some of them quite independent, others more or less influenced by one another.[2] The composition of the various biblical books took place over a span of centuries, while the final assembly and reworking into a commonly accepted canon of writings was undertaken in approximately the 4th century B.C.,[3] the purpose being to reverentially preserve each of them and at the same time to emphasize that they are in agreement with one another. The result was a mosaic which was well executed on the whole and, when completed, made up a more or less continuous document.

As to the book of Genesis, critical biblical research has separated out three diverse, originally independent recountings of Israel's earliest history. One of them is easily distinguished from the other two by its abstract language, its impersonal style, its concern for classification, precise names and exact dates, as well as repetitious formulations and a generally clerical view of things. Researchers therefore assume that it was composed during a relatively late period in Israel's history, probably the 6th to 5th century B.C., during or after the Babylonian exile. It is anonymous, like nearly all writings of the ancient Orient and the Bible, and is called the Priestly code (P) because its entire composition is permeated by a spirit reminiscent of that of the priesthood in the days of early Judaism.[4]

It is this late Priestly writing which gives us the first report of Creation, "In the beginning . . . " (Genesis 1–2:4). The second report, quite different from the first, deals with the creation of mankind in the Garden of Eden and its Fall (Genesis 2:5–3:24) and derives from a much older document, the author of which is known as the Yahwist because he usually refers to the God of Israel by the specific name of YHWH.[5] The third author/redactor

---

[2]J. Bottéro, "Jüdische Schöpfungsmythen" (Jewish Creation Myths), in *Quellen des alten Orients* (Sources of the Ancient Orient), Vol. I. Einsiedeln: Benziger, 1964, p. 185.
[3]*Biblisches Nachschlagewerk* (Biblical Reference Book). Stuttgart: Württembergische Bibelanstalt, 1964, p. 12.
[4]J. Bottéro, "Jüdische Schöpfungsmythen" (Jewish Creation Myths), p. 186.
[5]The discovery that Genesis 1 and Genesis 2ff. are derived from different sources was first made by the German pastor H. B. Bitter (1711) and the French physician J. Astruc (1753); this realization provided the impetus for modern Old Testament scholarship (O. H. Steck, *Die Paradieserzählung* (The Tale of Paradise), in the series "Biblische Studien," Neukirchener Verlag, 1970, p. 19).

is termed the Elohist, since he uses the more general term *Elohim* in referring to God.

It is generally thought today that the writings of the Elohist begin with the tale of Abraham the Patriarch (Genesis 12ff). The Yahwist (Y) and the scribe of the Priestly writings (P) saw things from a loftier vantage point and followed them back to the beginnings of mankind and the world, which is why they both start their accounts with a tale of creation.[6]

Present-day scholars unanimously ascribe the story of Paradise, with which we are primarily concerned here, to the Yahwist. Its writing is generally thought to have taken place in the 10th to 9th century B.C., the time of the Solomonic enlightenment or shortly thereafter, a period in which many old sacral traditions were in a state of crisis.[7] It is considered the oldest document in the Bible. But even here, scholars have uncovered inconsistencies and contradictions. It is believed that the Yahwist had a difficult time molding his material, because he was trying to harmonize various traditions within a single story.

Old Testament scholars continue to wonder and put forward hypotheses about the diverse oral traditions and mythological tales from which the Yahwist writer put together his account of Paradise.[8] It has often been remarked that there is no mention of the sea in the Yahwist account and that fish are missing from the enumeration of creatures created by YHWH (Genesis 2:19ff). For this reason it is thought that the original home of this myth might have been the southern and eastern parts of Palestine, where plains and farmlands lay practically side by side.

It is also possible that this myth goes back to nomads or semi-nomads, for the tree-rich Garden to the east probably was situated in the middle of the desert and, with its "flood [that] went up from the earth," sounds very much like an oasis. On the other hand, since the Genesis tale also names the rivers Tigris and Euphrates, its Palestinian origins would seem at first glance to be very questionable. It is also assumed that the other two rivers mentioned, Pishon and Gihon, actually refer to the two arms of a mighty

[6]Bottéro, "Judische Schöpfungsmythen" (Jewish Creation Myths), pp. 186–187.
[7]G. von Rad, "Das erste Buch Mose," cited in H. Haag, *Der Mensch am Anfang* (Mankind at the Beginning), p. 3.
[8]See, for example, ibid. and O. H. Steck, *Die Paradieserzählung* (The Tale of Paradise).

watercourse that was thought to encircle the world from both sides, with Mesopotamia as midpoint.[9] This cosmic river, which surrounds the earth like the waters around an island, is highly reminiscent of *Apsu*, the "earth ocean," about which much is to be found in the cosmological texts of Ancient Mesopotamia.[10]

It has often been noted that the passages concerning the four rivers (Genesis 2:11–14) could easily have been omitted without disturbing the continuity of the tale. In other words, they have all the earmarks of an interpolation. And the image of the oasis in the middle of the desert does not really fit into a landscape watered by four rivers. Hence the Yahwist story is thought to contain traces of two distinct traditions: a Palestinian myth about the origins of the world and mankind, and a Mesopotamian description of the geographic location, the latter colored by the cosmological image of an island surrounded by the world-ocean.

Far less obvious and clear is the origin of the Yahwist report on the creation of man and the animals. Both were formed from the earth, and man became a living being when God "breathed into his nostrils the breath of life." One is reminded here of the art of the potter or the sculptor of small statues, which touches slightly on some mythological concepts found in Mesopotamian writings.[11] As to the famous passage about the creation of woman from Adam's rib, J. Bottéro has offered the following comment: "Some light may be cast on the riddle of using man's rib as the springboard for creating woman . . . by resorting to something which has been known for a long time, namely, the existence of a Sumerian play on words for the two terms 'rib' and 'life,' both of which are represented by the same ideogram and pronounced *'ti* or *'til*. This could indicate some Mesopotamian influence [in the biblical tale], though to my knowledge no myth about the creation of mankind has been found in Mesopotamia which makes use of these homonyms."[12]

Moreover, thus far no myth has come to light from any other Middle Eastern land which mentions the creation of man and animals in the same sequence as that given in the Yahwist account.

[9]Bottéro, "Jüdische Schöpfungsmythen" (Jewish Creation Myths), p. 215.
[10]Ibid.
[11]Ibid., p. 216.
[12]Ibid.

In Genesis, man is there first of all (Genesis 2:7) and is put into the garden "to till it and keep it" (2:15). He is created as a solitary creature. Then the various forms of animal life are created, with the idea of providing man with company, since "It is not good that the man should be alone" (2:18). The man gives all the animals their names, "but for the man himself there was not found a helper fit for him" (2:20). This prompts God to provide that helper from the man's own body, forming it as a woman.

Some facets of this myth contain correspondences with Mesopotamian concepts about the creation of mankind: for example, man's initial hermaphroditic quality, which is reported in several ancient texts, or the idea that humanity was created in order to serve the gods or to complete Creation.[13]

But despite these parallels, the Yahwist account is highly original. Recent critical analysis[14] makes the assumption that the biblical tale of Paradise contains elements of a much older, probably oral tradition which speaks only of Adam and his exile from the Garden, while the elements of the serpent, Eve and the Tree of Life were injected by the Yahwist author. O. H. Steck[15] calls that more ancient tradition the "story of Paradise," in contrast to the complete "*tale* of Paradise" as set down by the Yahwist. At any rate, "here the Yahwist reworked a traditional tale and completed it his own way, following the same procedure he pursued elsewhere in the early history" of mankind.[16] This passage makes reference to the "Yahwist procedure" followed in writing down the tales of Cain and Abel, Noah and the flood, and the Tower of Babel, in which older traditional material was likewise reworked and supplemented.

Above all it is the monotheistic perspective of the Israelite religion which already informs the Yahwist tale of Paradise. In all other creation myths of the Ancient Orient, the history of the world begins with the birth of the gods themselves. The genesis of the gods is included in the genesis of the universe, and all gods are considered parts of the cosmos. But in the Book of Genesis,

[13]Ibid., pp. 216–217.
[14]Steck, *Die Paradieserzählung* (The Tale of Paradise).
[15]Ibid.
[16]Ibid., p. 56.

the Creator is master of his creation and not himself subject to any genetic process.

In the Book of Job, in Deutero-Isaiah and in certain Psalms, there are traces of the idea that YHWH too once had to fight the monster of chaos, Leviathan, as the hero Marduk struggles with the dragon of chaos Tiamat in the Babylonian creation myth.[17] But otherwise it is of the Old Testament essence that the Lord of Creation is the *only* god and stands above the cosmos which he has created.

Whatever the speculation and hypotheses about the origins of the biblical texts, it is regarded as certain today that traditional mythological motifs, having been taken up by the Israelites, were subjected to a process of substantive alteration before finally receiving their present form at the hand of the Yahwist author.[18] Many Old Testament scholars are of the opinion, in fact, that because of the transformation brought about through the Yahwist faith it is no longer appropriate to categorize the Genesis tale of Paradise and the Fall as a myth.[19]

Strictly speaking, this view may be justified given that a quantity of YHWH theology was obviously injected into the Yahwist's tale of Paradise. But from the psychological standpoint it seems to me legitimate to regard that tale, whether or not it is a myth in the strictest sense, as a self-consistent elaboration of mythological statement. In its present form it has engaged the minds and spirits of people of the Judeo-Christian culture for nearly three thousand years and has given rise to a great deal of faith, hope and also illusion. In addition to theological and philosophical speculation and interpretation, it has stimulated people's imagination to a broad range of artistic representation, in the course of which it has been constantly enriched with a vast diversity of imaginative contents. Hence it may be said to correspond to a necessity of the soul, expressing itself in archetypal images inherent in human nature. Its significance can never be totally plumbed, since it calls for new dimensions of comprehension for every age, every generation, and ultimately for every individual.

[17]V. Maag, "Syrien—Palästina" (Syria—Palestine) in Schmökel, *Kulturgeschichte des alten Orients* (Cultural History of the Ancient Orient), p. 79.
[18]H. Haag, *Der Mensch am Anfang* (Mankind at the Beginning), p. 3.
[19]Ibid.

4. Interpretive Efforts by the Church Fathers

By late Antiquity, the Church fathers were already intensively considering the question of whether the Genesis report of Paradise and the Fall was to be taken literally or allegorically.

The Hellenized Jewish philosopher Philo of Alexandria (13 B.C. to 40–50 A.D.) exerted great influence on the Church fathers' interpretation of the tale of Paradise. Philo tried to synthesize the Bible's revelation-based faith and the perceptions of Greek philosophy. He wanted the tale of Paradise to be understood symbolically rather than concretely. His reasoning provided an interpretive model which was to have great consequences for all future times. His symbolic interpretation was tantamount to a description of human "psychology" as it was then understood.[1]

For Philo, Paradise was a garden of virtues which God has planted in the human soul. This "garden" corresponds to Reason, which for Philo was the guiding attribute of the soul. And, as a garden is full of plants, so Reason is full of countless virtues. The Tree of Life indicates the greatest of all virtues, fear of God, by means of which the soul is made immortal, while the Tree of Knowledge of Good and Evil symbolizes the most central of virtues, insight, which differentiates things natural from things which are opposed to nature.

The Garden of Eden was situated in the east (the place of sunrise) because Reason never rests but constantly rises and illuminates the nighttime of the soul as the sun illuminates the darkness of the air.[2] The four rivers of Paradise were equated by

[1]R. Grimm, *Paradisus coelestis, Paradisus terrestris* (Celestial Paradise, Earthly Paradise). Munich: W. Fink Verlag, 1977, p. 24.
[2]Ibid.

Philo with the four cardinal virtues enumerated by Greek philosophy: wisdom, courage, moderation and justice.[3] Along with this symbolic, "psychological" interpretation, Philo also accepts the validity of certain literal interpretations, so that in part of his work he seems to strongly affirm the concrete existence of Paradise.[4]

The Church father Origen (b. 185 A.D. in Alexandria, d. 253–4 in Tyre) was a leading advocate of an exclusively allegorical view of Paradise. At the same time, however, he acknowledged the existence of a concrete Beyond, which he equated with the dwelling place of saved souls Jesus had promised to the meek of this world. The heavenly Paradise of which Origen wrote is to be understood tangibly; Origen admitted its invisibility but by no means its incorporeality.[5]

Also worth mentioning in this context is Ambrosius (340–397 A.D.), Bishop of Milan, who tried to link details from Genesis with cosmic principles from the world of neo-Platonic ideas. He saw Adam as the *nous*, the spiritual principle, while Eve was connected to *sensus*, the sensual aspect of life, and the spring which waters Paradise he equated with Jesus Christ as the source of life eternal or of God's wisdom.[6]

But there were also equally prominent representatives of fundamentalist views and the literal interpretation of Genesis, who objected mightily to allegorical interpretations, especially that of Origen. The evidence almost invariably cited for the correctness of a concrete, literal interpretation is the possibility of geographically localizing the four rivers of Paradise.

According to Tertullian (160–225 A.D., Carthage) there can be no denying the existence of an earthly Paradise. He describes it as surrounded by a zone of fire and removed from the rest of the world's knowledge. Here the earthly Paradise is linked to ancient Greek concepts of the Elysian Fields. Moreover, the passage in Genesis 2:16 is to be understood quite literally: The first humans did indeed eat actual food. And since Adam's exile, Paradise has continued to exist, serving as a temporary abode for saints, and especially martyrs, after their death.[7]

[3]Ibid., p. 26.
[4]Ibid., p. 31.
[5]Ibid., p. 37.
[6]Ibid., p. 50.
[7]Ibid., p. 45.

5. Augustine and the Doctrine of Original Sin

Aurelius Augustinus (354–430 A.D.), regarded as the true founder of Western attempts at Genesis interpretation, tries to link the symbolic and literal modes. He accepts Philo's equating of Paradise with the human soul, with the springs of Eden representing divine consolation watering the soul of mankind. In another allegorical effort, he sees Paradise as the Church itself, with the four rivers being the four Evangelists, and the fruit-bearing trees standing for the saints and their fruitful work.[1] But Augustine also transmits literal interpretations; he assumes that the earthly Paradise lies to the east, that it remains inaccessible to man and is probably situated on a mountain, since the Great Flood never reached it.

But most important are Augustine's statements about the condition of the first man in the earthly Paradise, since they constitute the foundation for his doctrine of Original Sin and all its many ramifications. He believed that Adam and Eve were mortal in Paradise and that they fed themselves with earthly fruits; if they had not violated God's commandment, after expiration of their life span they would have received the *corpus spirituale* (spirit body) and would then have enjoyed life eternal in the Resurrection.

The following bit of speculation is particularly interesting and enlightening: Adam was created in the full flower of his manhood, which would be the equivalent of roughly 30 years of age. Since

[1]Grimm, *Paradisus coelestis, Paradisus terrestris* (Celestial Paradise, Earthly Paradise), p. 60.

5. Rectangular Mandala with Cross, in the middle of which is the Lamb of God, surrounded by the four Evangelists and the four Springs of Paradise. In the four medallions are represented the four Cardinal Virtues, wisdom, courage, moderation and justice.

Zwiefalten Monastery, Brevier 12th C.

the first humans were initially created mortal in the *corpus animale* (animal body), there would have been the possibility of sexual relations between them *in* Paradise, if the Fall and the exile from Eden had not intervened. But the Fall brought a change in sexuality, introducing the element of sexual desire. Augustine wanted to show that sexual relations are possible without desire and developed in great detail a theory of marriage in Paradise.[2] Procreation and birth would have taken place without desire and without pain in Paradise, and the generations would not have followed one another but coexisted, since the fruit of the Tree of Life would have prolonged man's span. The sex organs would then have served their purpose without *voluptas* and *ardor* (instinctual lust) and there would have been no dissonance between rational will and instinct or between drive and ability.[3]

From the psychological standpoint it should be remarked here that Augustine's theory aims at paradisial "unitary reality" through the elimination of the conflict between instinct and will-as-reason. This is to take place at the cost of instinctuality, which is "sent to the devil," that is, demonized and repressed as much as possible so that it may cause no more dissonance in Paradise. At the same time this lends to the interpretation of the Fall a distinctly sexual tone which is not necessarily implicit in the original text.[4]

The theory of the marriage in Paradise, Augustine's wishful thinking about a controlled sexuality, became the foundation of medieval sexual ethics. It also served as the basis for an erotic utopianism which was based on the difference between the *gaudium* (joy) of Paradise and the *voluptas* (desire) of the post-paradisial world and which had considerable consequences for popular medieval literature.[5]

In any case, Augustine defended the idea that human guilt derives from Original Sin and the involvement of all mankind in Adam's downfall. These ideas generated a serious dispute between Augustine and Pelagius of Britain, who denied that Adam had left man a legacy of sin. In 1546 the Council of Trent came down on

---

[2]Ibid., p. 66.
[3]Ibid.
[4]Haag, *Der Mensch am Anfang* (Mankind at the Beginning), p. 56, footnote 129.
[5]R. Grimm, "Die Paradiesesehe, eine erotische Utopie des Mittelalters" (The Paradisial Marriage, a Medieval Erotic Utopia), in *Festschrift W. Mohr* (Göppinger Arbeiten zur Germanistik, 65). Göppingen: 1972.

the side of Augustine, issued its decree on Original Sin and confirmed for the medieval Christian world the direct connection between humanity's sinfulness and the sin of Adam. As recently as 1968 Pope Paul VI issued a "Credo" reiterating the doctrine as follows:

> Human Nature is [thus] a fallen nature, robbed of the Grace which once adorned it, wounded in its own natural forces and subject to the dominion of Death, which has been extended to all mankind. In this sense every human being is born in Sin. We therefore maintain, following the Council of Trent, that Original Sin is transmitted along with Human Nature through reproduction and not merely through emulation, and that it is thus inherent in each individual.[6]

There are quite a few myths, notably African ones, in which Paradise is lost through an oversight, the violation of some prohibition or other, through curiosity or some similar negative act or attitude. In these cases, too, the loss of Paradise is seen as the retribution of the gods. H. Baumann writes:

> These myths may well be called "legends of the Fall," as long as we do not use the term "sin" in an exclusively Christian sense. "Sin" is something well known to every primitive, if we understand it to mean the violation of a divine or social law. The fact that violation is always accompanied by punishment brings the concept very close to the European idea of sin, without there being any question of influence by European moral ideas.[7]

The Golden Age of the Greeks was also lost through human guilt, by means of what the Greeks called *hubris*. Meaning excessive pride, or arrogance, the term was used to designate an attitude or mode of behavior which, because of overweening pride or arrogance, overstepped the bounds of the divine order. A classic example is provided in the myth of Prometheus, who stole

---

[6]Pope Paul VI, Credimus 31, 33; 1968; translated here from the citation in J. Illies, *Die Sache mit dem Apfel* (The Business with the Apple). Freiburg im Breisgau: Herder, 1972, pp. 20–21.
[7]*Schöpfung und Urzeit des Menschen in Mythus der afrikanischen Volker* (Creation and the Primal Era of Mankind in the Mythology of African Peoples), pp. 267ff.

fire from the gods in order to give it to man. As a punishment he was chained to a mountain in the Caucasus, where an eagle fed on his liver. The gods devised yet another punishment for mankind when they created the first woman and sent her down to earth. She was Pandora, out of whose untimely opened box flew all the ills that beset humanity. These myths were recounted by Hesiod in his *Works and Days* in an effort to explain the difficulties of human existence.

It is hardly necessary to underscore the striking similarity between these ideas of ancient Greece and the biblical tale of Paradise. In our context, however, it would be of particular interest to examine the idea of Original Sin from the standpoint of depth psychology. From that perspective the doctrine would seem to have its own justification.

6. The Psychological View of Original Sin

To come into this world inevitably means to take on guilt. It is not possible to exist without becoming tangled in guilt in some form or other. The very act of being born causes great pain to one's mother. Many steps along the path to maturity, which involve a gradual release from parental authority, cause our parents disappointment and suffering—a guilt which we must simply accept. Often we find that we cannot return the intense love offered to us by another, and thus we become guilty of causing that person pain. Whether intentionally or unintentionally, our spontaneous remarks may strike vulnerable spots in others. Out of self-defense or other concerns, lies become unavoidable in some situations. Behind every basically "good" deed there is a mixture of noble and less noble motives, such as self-righteousness, the desire for prestige, etc. Kant's "categorical imperative" of pure ethics violates human nature. There is "shadow" in every aspect of our lives. It is difficult to argue with St. Paul when he says: "I do not do the good I want, but the evil I do not want is what I do" (Romans 7:19). These are facts of human existence, with which we must deal whether we like it or not.

Paradise, on the other hand, is the idea of an existence in innocence. It is interesting to note that in the Genesis tale the animals are not driven out of Paradise—with the exception of the accursed serpent. The beasts appear to live in paradisial innocence, even those predators who survive by catching their prey alive and cruelly dismembering and eating it. Catching prey, however, is a condition of their existence as laid down in the plan of Creation. They are not conscious of what it does. This is why reference is so often made to "innocent children." In terms of their behavior, infants are often anything but harmless; not infrequently they are almost demonic, since they are unaware of the ethical virtue of consideration for others. But we do not hold them responsible for their acts, since they do not recognize the implications of their existence. And so we say that they live in innocence.

It is clearly the general consensus that guilt arises only where there is the possibility of *awareness* of guilt. When a glimmer of the idea of good and evil is perceived, the child's paradisial existence in innocence is immediately forfeited. We are faced here with an extremely complex phenomenon. The *awareness* of guilt is based on conscience, which in turn arises from our feelings of guilt (what Freud termed "the anxiety of conscience"). These are extremely unpleasant signals which are perceived when our acts are not in harmony with our conscience. They often crop up even when we merely think, wish for or fantasize about something which our conscience deems "bad."

Some psychological observations about the problem-complex of conscience and guilt might be in order at this point: In the Genesis tale of Paradise the first impetus toward the Fall is provided by doubt. The perfection of Paradise is called into question, and it is of course the serpent who plants the seed of doubt in mankind's ear. In Goethe's *Faust*, Mephistopheles, the opponent of God, refers to the serpent as his cousin: "Follow the adage of my cousin Snake. From dreams of god-like knowledge you will wake to fear, in which your very soul shall quake."[1] In the Christian tradition God's opponent is known as the Devil. In German the word is *Teufel*, derived from the Old German *tiufal*. Although not etymologically linked to the German word *Zweifel* (doubt), one might assume a certain klang-association between the two. But both *tiufal* and Devil are derived from the Latin *Diabolus*. That, in turn, developed from the Greek verb *diaballein*, which literally means "to throw into confusion" and was understood to connote "to bisect, to create enmity, to slander or insult." These connotations bring us back close to the German word for

[1] J. W. von Goethe, *Faust*, Part I, translated by Philip Wayne. Penguin Classics. Harmondsworth, Middlesex: Penguin Books, 1949, p. 99.

"doubt," *Zweifel,* which originally was composed of two elements, *zwei* (two) and *fallen* (to fall). Interestingly, the English word "double" is etymologically related to the Old German and Old Frisian words for "doubt." In brief, then, "to doubt" connotes "to fall into two parts" or "to fall out of an initial unity" or "to waver in the face of two possibilities."[2]

The serpent thus symbolizes, among other things, human nature's inherent potentiality for doubting, for calling things into question. The snake "poisons" the satisfaction of a complacent harmony with some sort of order, whether external or internal; it represents a deep-seated human instinct to eventually cast doubt on the validity of taboos, articles of faith and value systems. It therefore stands for "Evil" from the vantage point of those external or internal systems of order. But from the standpoint of life's ongoing flux, calling things into question is positive and necessary; doubt gives rise to new orientation.

However it is viewed, the serpent in Paradise is *impulse.* It may be "Part of a power that would alone work evil, but engenders good."[3] But it may also be a mad temptation to the *hubris* of "god-like knowledge"[4] and thus an impulse to catastrophe (viz., the Third Reich under Hitler). In any case, though, the impulse generated by doubting what has been handed down is a prerequisite for the soul's vitality, no matter how many risks are involved. Anthropologist A. Gehlen has aptly termed man a "creature at risk."[5]

[2]Webster's *Third New International Dictionary, Unabridged.* Springfield, Mass.: G. & C. Merriam, 1969.
[3]Goethe, *Faust,* Part I, p. 75.
[4]Ibid., p. 99.
[5]A. Gehlen, *Der Mensch* (The Person). Bonn, 1955, p. 35.

7. On the Psychogenesis of Conscience

The research of child psychologist D. W. Winnicott has also indicated that doubt, cropping up in early childhood, is the first manifestation of a dawning moral sense. This point requires some elaboration: In an earlier chapter we observed that disturbances of the primal relationship during the first year of life are generally to be found at the root of pathological guilt feelings. The same early factor is often the source of a depressive conviction of one's own "badness." This leads to the conclusion that the root of what we term "conscience" goes back to the first year of a person's life.

Winnicott sees signs of a nascent conscience in the fact that, during the second half of its first year, an infant demonstrates what the psychologist terms "concern."[1] Winnicott has found evidence to support the view that the first signs of "concern" appear when the infant has attained a sufficient level of maturity to recognize its mother as an entire person and to notice that the "object mother" and the "environment mother" are united in one and the same individual.[2] Since the infant's love impulses toward the "object mother" are coupled with aggressive attacks (the school of thought following Melanie Klein, in what is perhaps an exaggerated view, holds that the infant believes it is eating the object and greedily taking possession of it), "concern" arises that it may also have destroyed the benevolent "environment mother." This also gives rise to the first doubt as to whether a

[1]D. W. Winnicott, *The Maturational Processes and the Facilitating Environment*. New York: International University Press, 1965, pp. 73ff.
[2]Ibid., p. 40.

natural, spontaneous acting out of instinctual impulses in "paradisial innocence" may not be only good but may also have a destructive side. For the first time, spontaneous, natural impulsivity is called into question, which leads to a preconscious, dimly perceived dichotomy of Good and Evil.

At first glance this train of thought may seem excessively speculative, particularly because complex psychic processes are being ascribed to the "unknowing" infant. But the doubt-filled anxiety that "hate will be greater than love"[3] must have its origin in man's inherent proclivity to be a social creature. Doubts about whether the mother has been destroyed by aggressive attacks are linked to the fear of losing her and of being left alone, bereft of the mother who creates the benevolent, supportive environment upon which the infant is totally dependent. Ultimately, behind it all, is the fear that the plan for life and development implanted in the child's self may not be realized.

In this phase the absence of the mother is itself a threat to life. Of course, the infant knows nothing of this threat or of any "development plan"—it is simply guided by the latter, living it instinctively without the ability to reflect upon it. But seen from the perspective of this plan for life and the development of consciousness, the categories of Good and Evil (as a kind of "primal knowledge") seem linked to the fact that love and bond-creating attitudes are more valuable than hatred and aggression. Although aggressivity in the sense of "staking out territory" has its value for ego development and self-maintenance, a predominance of bond-creating love is essential to life, both in mankind and in the animal kingdom.[4]

On the basis of long experience and observation, Winnicott arrived at the conclusion that the ethical sense develops naturally in a human being rather than being primarily imposed from the outside. The doubt which gives rise to "concern," in the sense of a caring sense of responsibility, is inherent in the human psyche, but it needs a maturation period of at least six months in the infant's life before it can manifest itself. The development of consciousness is inherent as a potentiality in human nature, and

[3]Ibid., p. 21.
[4]See, for example, Irenäus Eibl-Eibesfeldt, *Love and Hate: The Natural History of Behavior Patterns.* New York: Holt, Rinehart & Winston, 1972.

the subliminal doubt as to whether spontaneous action is "good" (i.e., loving) or "bad" (i.e., destructive) is an important landmark along the path of maturation. The serpent, symbol of the first doubt to arise in the Paradise of the unitary reality, provides the impetus leading to the question of Good and Evil and to its consequence, the loss of that early Paradise.

But to insure that the doubt does not lead to despair[5]—as often happens in cases of a disturbed primal relationship—the empathic presence of the mother-figure as "facilitating environment" is essential. It is of decisive importance that the infant's fear of having destroyed the mother not appear to come true, that the mother remain present as a caring and supportive "other." The infant needs time for reparation and restoration of a loving relatedness.

Infants, of course, have their ways of appealing, their smiles, gurgles, etc. These are signals which stimulate maternal attention and the impulse to bodily contact. When the mother is still there after "attacks" and responds to her child's gestures of reparation, order is restored to the infant's sense of self and world. The mother is then seen to be not "destroyed," but accepting of the ambivalence of natural, spontaneous action. Such an experience is fundamental for the child, helping it to accept the mixture of good and evil, love and hate, in the spontaneous impulses of the soul, and eventually to take responsibility for all of it. This is the basis of what Neumann calls an "integral ego."

Neumann also rightly points out that the experience of the primal relationship can be expressed in the infantile formula: "As your mother loves you to be, so should you be."[6] This formula is significant on many levels. Maternal empathy means the ability of the mother (or mother-figure) to feel her way into the infant's vital need for care; it means being in harmony with those natural needs of the child which are basic to its maturational processes. In this way the infant's primal experience of harmony is confirmed, and "the child's innate order accords with the order implemented by its mother. The child's experience of a loving harmony with a higher order which at the same time corresponds

[5]In the German language the word for doubt is *Zweifel*; the word for despair is *Verzweiflung*, clearly built around the same root.—*Trans.*
[6]Erich Neumann, *The Child*, p. 90.

to its own nature is the first foundation of a morality that does not do violence to the individual but allows him to develop in a process of slow growth."[7] In other words, a mother who is capable of harmonizing her feelings and actions with her child's internal realities and needs and does not impose external training measures prematurely, encourages the child's essential ability to be able at a later time in its life to listen to its own inner voice, the "voice of conscience." That conscience is felt as a sense of guilt whenever there is a deviation from that primal order—which happens again and again, and which indeed must happen by virtue of the ego's freedom. This form of conscience might be termed the "guardian of the ego-self axis." By means of guilt feelings, it sounds the alarm whenever the intentions of ego-consciousness deviate too far from the primal order of human existence (the *self*, in the Jungian sense of the word).

According to Winnicott, the need to make restitution also has its roots in the primal relationship. The need to make amends after committing a "bad" act seems to be an archetypal component of the human psyche, and is reflected in the almost universal presence of purification rites in the human cultures (including the confessional in the Catholic church). Psychoanalytical writers have repeatedly pointed out that there is in the psyche a tendency to self-punishment, the purpose of which is to set things straight once again. Reconciliation following an argument with another person generally brings a momentary sense of happiness. To be irreconcilable means to insist on one's own rightness and innocence, to deny one's own share of the guilt. But for the most part people feel a basic need (a concern) to make things "all right" again.

It now becomes possible to understand in an even more differentiated manner why disturbances of the primal relationship can result in deep-seated, unrealistic and destructive guilt feelings—indeed, guilt complexes. If a mother is not sufficiently empathic and does not give her child time to make reparations, the infant's doubt may turn into despair (*Zweifel* into *Verzweiflung*) that its spontaneous impulses are wicked and destructive.

[7]Ibid., p. 91.

This also means that the child's innate order is not in harmony, but in conflict, with the order represented by the mother-as-world. It means falling out of the paradisial unitary reality—*not*, as natural development would have it, into a world in which the effort of "being good" can compensate somewhat for its opposite, "being bad," but rather expelled into the hell of those who are *only* bad, where there is no redemption through reparation.

An example from my own practice might serve to illustrate these connections. A 26-year-old patient dreamed that she lay abandoned and imprisoned in a dark dungeon, hounded by a voice which called incessantly: "You are damned. You are guilty. All is lost." But when she listened more closely she suddenly realized that it was "only" the voice of her mother and she felt greatly relieved.

This woman was plagued by depressions and the concomitant underlying feeling that everything that was in her and expressed by her was bad, or at least "laughable." She rejected all of her own psychic spontaneity, her feelings, thoughts and impulses, and experienced everyone around her as rejecting too. In her own eyes she was one of the damned.

In her relationship to me, her therapist, she was extremely shy, hardly daring to expose herself in any way. But since I was empathic toward her and cautiously formulated what I thought she must be feeling and what I could see of her inner life through her dreams, she felt herself to be understood. And this feeling of being understood awakened in her an old, never-fulfilled longing for unitary reality in the primal relationship. The longing was projected onto me in the transference, which at the same time caused the woman extremely painful feelings of guilt. Naturally she did not dare to speak of all this and withheld those dreams that dealt with her feelings for me, which only intensified her guilt feelings. As a result, there was a progressive blockage of the interaction between us.

Our relationship grew tense, until I gently mentioned my hunch that she might be feeling a need to get closer to me but that this need was at the same time a source of anxiety, shame and guilt. I also pointed out that she was probably afraid of being rejected if she were to express her feelings. Blushing but evidently relieved, she nodded as I spoke, while I added that such feelings were natural, important and valuable.

After that she gradually became somewhat freer and a bit more spontaneous. One day she was even able to express the fantasy that it would be Paradise for her to be near me day and night, to cook for me and care for me; at the same time, she said, she felt strong feelings of hatred toward me because I was denying her the fulfillment of that wish. Finally, she expressed intense envy of me because I was so "perfect" and my life was so much better than hers.

I was deeply gratified that she had dared to articulate her fantasies. But it was too much for her. After our session she fell into a depression and was convinced that she had now destroyed all the good she had gotten from me and that she was the most ungrateful, miserable, importunate of human beings. It was inconceivable to her that I would be unchanged in our next session and she fully expected abuse, disgrace and rejection—which she felt she deserved.

She came to our next meeting sullen, without a word of greeting. When I remarked, "It seems to me that you're afraid you shattered me as well as our good relationship in your last session," her tongue was loosened. Out came self-accusations about her "impossible" behavior, how hopelessly bad and spoiled she was. I told her that I could understand her fears and guilt feelings, and that I suspected it was not the first time she had felt the need of such self-castigation after letting slip some spontaneous feelings, impulses or fantasies. This triggered a flood of memories about her mother, and it soon became evident to what an extent the things she was now experiencing in her relationship to me were a repetition of countless scenes with her mother. Such memories, of course, are not of the very early infancy period of which Winnicott speaks; they are memories of later repetitions based on a pattern of experience which has its foundation in early infancy.

The fact that I, as a sympathetic other, was still "there" after all that had transpired, that she had not in fact destroyed all the "good" which I represented, was a source of some relief to my analysand. Moreover she was now able to willingly give me a great deal of information about her early experiences which had come up in memory, thus giving me a gift which I obviously wanted—a rough equivalent of the "reparation" experience.

Such episodes were repeated often, and it became increasingly clear to her that her belief in damnation to her own private hell did not stem from some divine judgment. In her dream cited previously the seemingly omnipotent voice, the goddess pronouncing the curse upon her, had turned out to be her own personal mother. This served to relativize the absoluteness of her belief in her own damnation. A mother is, after all, someone with whom a person can contend in adulthood; she is no longer equated with the "world order," as she is experienced in infancy. The projection by which the personal mother is seen as the Great Mother whose "attitude is the supreme judgment"[8] can be withdrawn.

The example we have just looked at illustrates how a person can find himself caught in a hell of tortured conscience in later life unless he has learned that his anxieties about having destroyed the mother, and hence being abandoned and bad, are unfounded because that same mother is still sympathetically there for him and accepts his efforts at reparation.

Primary guilt complexes of this kind are so painful partly because their origins are so indefinable. One does not know what the "crimes" really are, about which one feels so unavoidably guilty. And so, concrete "sins" must be found. Every confessor knows of people who, after each confession, feel powerful scruples as to whether they have been truly honest and kept nothing back. As a rule they manage to find some unconfessed transgression about which they return to the confessional. No absolution can reassure them that they have really made reparation for their guilt and that their relation to the divine, the world and themselves is once again in order.

Interestingly enough, asocial and delinquent behavior (especially among youth) frequently stems from the same source, as Freud pointed out: "Analytical work then brought the surprising discovery that such acts were done principally *because* [my italics] they were forbidden, and because their execution was accom-

---

[8]Ibid., p. 87.

panied by mental relief to their doer. He was suffering from an oppressive feeling of guilt of which he did not know the origin, and after he had committed a misdeed this oppression was mitigated. His sense of guilt was at least attached to something."[9] When "despair" has been generated in earliest childhood because attempts at reparation have not been accepted, the result in later life may be an unconscious need for punishment. This in turn reflects the unconscious hope that, by being punished, reparation can finally be made and thus order and peace be restored with oneself and with the world.

In relatively rare cases the ability to experience guilt feelings, which are based on "concern," may remain undeveloped or be lost. It has not yet been conclusively proven whether such a lack of rudimentary conscience is a congenital anomaly or whether severe deprivation in early infancy has prevented the individual from ever achieving the emotional level of "concern."

An interesting dream experienced by a cold-blooded murderer is cited in a study by M.-L. von Franz.[10] It was a frequently recurring dream and therefore may be assumed to have depicted the dreamer's characteristic psychic situation. In it the man found himself at a country fair where there were many swings. He mounted one of the swings and began swinging back and forth, higher and higher. Suddenly he swung so high that he shot out into empty space. Each time this dream recurred, the dreamer would awaken without any emotional reaction, neither anxiety nor terror.

The dream shows that, on the emotional level, this man cannot take seriously the polarities of high and low, forward and backward, ultimately of good and evil; instead he simply swings back and forth between them (much as opportunistic politicians seesaw between positions). As a consequence he leaves the gravity field of "Mother Earth" and is lost out in space. But even this awakens neither fear nor anxiety in him; he seems to be utterly without fear and without "concern." He simply drops out of the realm of earth-centered human existence, without any apparent

[9]Freud, *The Complete Psychological Works*. Standard Edition. London: Hogarth Press, 1973, Vol. 14, p. 332.
[10]M. L. von Franz, *Shadow and Evil in Fairytales*. Zurich: Spring Publications, 1974.

reaction. All those emotions which bind human beings to one another, which center and bind the individual personality within itself—graphically symbolized in the dream by earth's field of gravity—seem to be missing in him.

The concern over having destroyed the mother, over being bad and destructive, which crops up for the first time in late infancy, is primarily linked to the fear that, by incurring such guilt, one will be left alone and helpless when the mother is no longer present. Thus, to be loving and good is in keeping with one's own basic needs and survival instinct; to be destructive and bad is self-damaging. These are quasi-instinctual elements in the earliest developmental phase of the moral sense.

Morality may thus be seen not as altruistic and selfless, but rather as closely linked to the survival instinct and its concerns. Since humanity is by nature a social species, a *zoon politikon* as Aristotle put it, there must be inherent in it in some rudimentary form the disposition to harmonize the needs of personal survival with the needs of the social group. This harmonization is brought about in good measure by our sense of responsibility, our conscience, the earliest form of which is the infant's "concern."

Understood as sympathetic caring, this "concern" is certainly the foundation of later consideration for other people and their integrity. The inconsiderate acting out of one's own instinctual needs does violence to other people; in some circumstances it may result in severe antisocial behavior. To be loved and esteemed within one's family, professional group and broader social circle—which is a fundamental requirement for self-esteem—the individual needs "concern" in the form of responsible attention to an instinct-limiting code of behavior. A person is tactful, considerate, helpful and sympathetic because his or her own self-esteem depends to a great extent on love and social esteem.

From this perspective every good deed also has its "selfish" motive. Pure altruism is humanly impossible; it is always mixed with the need for self-gratification. This fact might perhaps also be characterized as "original sin." Becoming conscious of it, looking it squarely in the eye, may help to safeguard us from a dubious sense of moral self-righteousness. But its consequence in the matter of conscience raises a problem which will be touched upon later.

What Winnicott has termed "concern" and tagged as the foundation of man's innate conscience is, however, also related to the fear of falling out of an enveloping whole, out of harmony with a higher level of order—a falling out that is experienced as "bad" on a primary level. The sense of containment in that higher order, which is first represented by the mother, is also the root of subsequent religious faith. The infant's experience that efforts at restitution can lead to harmony with a higher order (which at that stage embraces mother, world and self) is the root of a later religious trust in a Divinity (in whatever form it may be conceived).

Thus "concern" is also carried over into the religious realm, as the careful attention to a knowledge and will which are supraordinated to the individual ego and make themselves known through the voice of conscience.

8. The God of Paradise

How are we to comprehend, from a psychological standpoint, the deity who reigns in Paradise?

In our Judeo-Christian mythology the Lord of Creation seems concerned that the humans he fashioned feel comfortable in his world. He permits them to do whatever they please, with the exception of one restriction, the ban against eating the fruit of the Tree of Knowledge. Thus primal mankind lives in harmony with God, nature and its own natural creatureliness. The God of the paradisial world does not seem to be the same deity as the one who later hands down the Tablets of the Law at Sinai and so imposes a code of conduct on his people.[1]

At the risk of plunging into a hornets' nest of divergent theological and religious-historical doctrines, I would venture the psychological interpretation that the God of Paradise may be understood as the ordering factor, the principle of structure in nature, more or less as the center of natural, biopsychic regulation.

Like the beasts, a human infant lives in "unity with nature," which is why it is regarded as "innocent." Active within it, however, are structural determinants, some of which are functionally aimed at survival and others at promoting the processes of maturation. The effects of these determinants, in turn, are dependent on empathic reactions from the mother. But behind

[1] I am not speaking here in a theological sense, nor do I propose to delve into the historical reasons for these diverse images of God. My concern is simply to underscore the existence of such differences and to examine their psychological significance.

139

the archetype of the Great Mother (understood as "nature" in the broadest sense), which is graphically symbolized by the Garden of Paradise in which everything grows and flourishes, is the voice of the Creator and Organizer of all nature's splendors.

As a "unitary reality," Paradise is characterized by a state of being in which spirit and nature are not polar opposites. Spirit, as the creative, ordering and meaning-giving principle, is incarnate in nature. The rule of nature has its own inherent sense and structure; in fact, it is through nature and the wisdom of the natural regulatory principles inherent in all creatures that the workings of the creative Divinity can be perceived. In mankind this is notably the case with respect to each human's fundamental bio-psychic needs, which are most clearly observable during infancy and early childhood.

The spirit in nature expresses itself especially in what C. G. Jung termed "absolute knowledge."[2] It manifests itself in the ingenious structures of all life forms, through which life seeks to regulate itself. In the physiological realm this regulation is known as homeostasis (i.e., internal stability or balance). The human body, for example, must maintain a very constant temperature, and its cells require constant nourishment with sugar. Processes in which such factors as blood sugar, blood pressure and body temperature must be kept constant are termed homeostatic, because they involve complex adjustments which maintain a steady balance, compensating for any variations and external influences. These physiological processes are largely unconscious, beyond the range of ego-awareness. We perceive them only when something in the overall process fails to function properly. This is brought to our attention in the form of pain or discomfort, so that the vital striving for homeostasis is extended into our consciousness. Certain processes, however, are of necessity registered consciously—e.g., hunger, the signal that nourishment is to be taken in order to maintain biological stability.

In other words, the extremely complex physiology of the human body "knows" how it must function in order to maintain life. And it had this knowledge long before human consciousness,

[2]*Collected Works*, Vol. 8

in the form of science, observed these processes and described their "laws." Aside from the stomach, which knows when it is hungry, there is, among other things, the sex drive, which knows how it must make us behave if the human species is not to die out. Consciousness and the ability to reflect—two specifically human traits—are likewise inherent in our species; that is, there must be in nature some kind of "knowing" which equips humans with the capacity to become conscious.

In the biblical myth of Paradise, the "voice of God that spoke in the Garden" (to which Neumann also refers as " the individual experience of the transpersonal"[3]) is heard in the call: "Adam, where are you?" It is perceived at the moment when an awareness of the polarity of Good and Evil has cropped up, along with its attendant feelings of guilt and shame. Before that time there was no call; no voice was needed, for the first humans had felt no impulse to hide. It is the divisive deviation from "innocent" identification with the "absolute knowledge" of nature that brings the birth of human ego-awareness. That is to say, the attainment of ego-consciousness requires a shattering of the unconsciousness of unitary reality.

To what extent God accepts the new fact that "the man has become like one of us, knowing good and evil," is difficult to say. It does not, at any rate, seem to be totally opposed to his creative intentions, or else in his omnipotence he could have restored the status quo ante. But his "voice" demonstrates the consequence of this sudden acquisition of consciousness: the loss of unitary reality and the sudden plunge into conflict-laden polarity. Human consciousness, which is founded on polarity and largely confined to polarities, can partake only to a very limited extent in the timeless and eternal, which is symbolized by the Tree of Life. Access to this lost mystery is guarded by the cherubim and the whirling, flashing sword. This image informs us that we must know of our own mortality, of our inevitable participation in the natural cycle of death and becoming, that we ourselves are not the masters over life and death.

The "voice" belongs to the Creator of all reality. To hear it

[3]See *The Origins and History of Consciousness*, p. 403.

therefore also means to have some sense of life's plan and of the power of natural wisdom in the human psyche. One of the ways the voice of that natural wisdom seeks to make itself heard is through certain dreams. To Goethe's dictum that "In the dark recesses of his soul the good man knows the proper path" might be added the idea that dreams, in endless variation, can illumine those dark recesses and make them accessible.

9. The God of the Decalogue

What does it mean to encounter not the God of Paradise, but the God of the Ten Commandments, the Lord of the "shalts" and "shalt nots," as he shows himself at Sinai? Neumann is surely right in stating: "When paradise is abandoned, the voice of God that spoke in the Garden is abandoned too, and the values of the collective, of the fathers, of law and conscience, of the current morality, etc., must be accepted as the supreme values in order to make social adaptation possible."[1]

Parallel to the development of consciousness, the development of conscience comes under the dominance of the father archetype. The code of behavior of what Neumann has termed "the partriarchal system of order" begins very early to have its effect on the young child. Whether spoken or unspoken, "Thou shalt" and "Thou shalt not" begin as soon as the child can move about on its own and develop activities independent of its parents. At that point it is necessary to learn the particular code of behavior transmitted by the child's familial environment, to accept that code as valid, to introject it, as the technical jargon has it. In other words, it is necessary to somehow harmonize the child's own nature with the demands of socialization. Since the child continues to be fundamentally dependent upon the love of its parents, the "concern" that this love might be lost through disobedience serves to promote the process of socialization.

The development of ego-centered, self-responsible consciousness liberated mankind from regulation by nature's absolute knowledge. As a result, humanity evidently needs the aid of

[1]Neumann, *The Origins and History of Consciousness*, p. 403.

norms and guidelines with which to orient its thinking, feeling and action. Unity with the God of Paradise, with "nature's creative knowing," must be relinquished in favor of a divinity who gives specific content to the generalized differentiation of Good and Evil as opposites.

In the Judeo-Christian tradition this divinity reveals itself primarily as God the Father, the principle of leadership and guidance: "I am the Lord your God, who brought you out of the land of Egypt, out of the house of bondage" (Exodus 20:2). He spreads awe and lays down conditions, commandments and laws. Only in the commandment regarding sanctification of the Sabbath is reference made to God the Creator, and then only harking back to the first biblical account of creation, that of the Priestly code.

The divine commandments provide clear guidelines for the behavior of the individual, especially within the social context. For his part, God the Father rewards obedience to his commandments with the promise to guide and protect his people. Obedience to God's commandments thus becomes the basic condition for the survival and well-being of the entire people. In other words: Valid guidelines backed by authority make possible an organized, more or less peaceable communal life, which is of vital importance both for the individual and for the collective. Thus the authority of the moral code ultimately serves the survival of the collective, upon which the individual in turn is dependent; it is, for humankind, an essential prerequisite for the survival of the individual and the species.

The link to the "absolute knowledge" in or behind all life is in this way maintained. Based as it is on polarity, however, our human consciousness often apprehends nature and spirit, Being and moral imperative, as conflicted opposites. (Freud took this fact into account in writing of the conflict between the instinctual drives of the Id and the moral demands of the Superego.) It is to the authority of the imperative, the moral code itself, that we must account for our relation to our instinctual existence, how we control and channel it. The moral code changes in the course of history, and differs significantly from culture to culture. But whatever its content, and no matter how often its rigidity may do violence to human nature, the need for such a moral code to exist is profoundly in keeping with "absolute knowledge," part of the essential, archetypal ground of the human species.

10. Moral Code, Superego and Conscience

The child comes up against the demands of the moral code, must adjust to it and introject it so that it becomes effective as the superego, the inner force of conscience. "The superego is the representative for us of every moral restriction, the advocate of the striving for perfection—it is, in short, as much as we have been able to grasp psychologically of what is described as the higher side of human life."[1] It speaks for "the interests of supra-individual reality in a human community as opposed to the interests of the individual."[2] Neumann refers to the superego as "another 'authority' within the personality [which] represents the collective conscious values, though these vary with the type of collective and its values, and also with the stage of consciousness which the collective has reached."[3]

The predisposition of the individual to develop as part of a community is inherent, an archetypal part of human nature. One of its aspects is the willingness to be molded and guided by the collectively accepted norms of the community. These norms are internalized early in life and experienced as one's own conscience. Accordingly, psychoanalysis came to the conclusion that conscience, understood as the demands of the child's superego, is formed not on the basis of the parents' lived-out example but rather on the basis of the parental superegos. This is because the parents pass along to the child their own idealized superego

---

[1]Freud, *The Complete Psychological Works*, Vol. 22, pp. 66–67.
[2]T. Uexküll, *Grundfragen der psychosomatischen Medizin* (Basic Questions of Psychosomatic Medicine). Munich: Rowohlt, 1968.
[3]*The Origins and History of Consciousness*, p. 364.

demands, which they in turn acquired in the confrontation with their own parents and teachers. Thus the superego becomes "the vehicle of tradition and of all the time-resisting judgments of values which have propagated themselves in this way from generation to generation."[4] This is why people never live entirely in the present: "The past, the tradition of the race and of the people, lives on in the ideologies of the super-ego, and yields only slowly to the influence of the present and to new changes."[5]

It is questionable to what extent these views of Freud's are still valid for today's world, with its relativization of traditional values. But he is certainly correct to the extent that, behind the desire to be "modern," the deep-seated traditional values tend to break out again at decisive moments. In their efforts to breed "new men" appropriate to their new ideologies, revolutionary regimes must resort to brutal techniques of re-education in order to root out old values embedded in the superego—and even then they never succeed completely.

In developing the concept of the superego, however, Freud did not intend to confine it only to those social norms introjected by each individual, as is often asserted. His realization that the super-ego is also the bearer of "time-resisting judgments" makes the question of conscience a far more complex matter even from the psychoanalytic standpoint. As he wrote: "What has belonged to the lowest part of the mental life of each of us is changed through the formation of the ideal, into what is highest in the human mind by our scale of values."[6]

In this way Freud attempted to formulate an empirical factor by which conscience may be recognized. There are always reactions of conscience which are diametrically opposed to the dominant collective consciousness and its value system—a clear sign that conscience cannot be invariably equated with the introjected values of the collective. After fifty years of indoctrination under an ideologically strict sociopolitical order, for example, individuals regularly arise whose consciences force them to express opposition to that system, even at enormous cost to themselves. This phenomenon has been manifested in all historical periods and

[4]Freud, *The Complete Psychological Works*, Vol. 22, p. 67.
[5]Ibid.
[6]Freud, *The Complete Psychological Works*, Vol. 19, p. 36.

often provides the impetus for social and cultural change. But the question might be raised of whether this "time-tested" aspect of the superego truly represents only the past and its traditions, as Freud interpreted the phenomenon, or whether it can be understood as a kind of regulatory authority which attempts to compensate extreme deviations from species-appropriate "human nature" and to loosen an excessively rigid adherence to a particular system of order.

We have thus put forward the hypothesis that there is an "authority" at work within us which strives to prevent the worst deviation from mankind's "humanity." It is, after all, a fact that we would be unable to develop any ethical concepts at all—and it is these which provide the orientation for conscience—if there were no inherent archetypal predisposition to do so.

This, however, brings us to the question of why conscience, which is an archetypal element in human nature, appears to permit situations in which mankind's ethical attitudes are rather dubious. If the moral code in the form of the superego were the sole internal source of guidance and control, punishing every deviation with painful guilt feelings, there would be no need for external institutions which maintain the social order by means of police forces and powerful sanctions. Yet, everywhere in the world, society must resort to such external sanctions in order to impose its moral code.

This is doubtless linked to the fact that the internalization of moral norms does not happen inevitably and automatically, but is based on complex developmental processes. The unreliability of the moral function may therefore be regarded as a symptom of a lack of psychic maturity. At the same time, the very fact that introjection of the moral code is not inevitable leaves a certain amount of leeway for possible manifestations of that inner voice of conscience which calls: "Adam, where are you?"

In this context, D. W. Winnicott has made the following interesting observation: "Where there is a lack of personal moral sense the implanted moral code is necessary, but the resultant socialization is unstable."[7] In other words, the personal moral sense is not necessarily identical with the externally imposed

[7] *The Maturational Processes and the Facilitating Environment*, p. 32.

moral code. But those two components of the empirically effective conscience *may* be identical in some instances—for example, when the value system advocated by a church genuinely harmonizes with a person's innermost conscience.

The conflict between an imposed moral code and a personal conscience which may manifest itself as an interior voice in the individual personality, has played an important part in human history. The oldest known document depicting an individual whose conscience is in a state of conflict with collective beliefs is an Egyptian papyrus known as "The Dialogue of a World-Weary Man With His Ba," of which a new translation with commentary was prepared some years ago by the Egyptologist Helmuth Jacobsohn.[8] The papyrus dates from the period around 2200 B.C. The world-weary man apparently has too much insight into the collective injustices of his time. He suffers from this and feels alienated, because he is too conscious for his contemporaries and sees too much. He wishes to commit suicide and turns to his "Ba" soul, a representation of his personal conscience, for advice.

For our purposes, one passage is of particular interest. The Ba-soul tells the world-weary man not to place too much importance on strict observance of the institutional rites of burial. This was a monstrously heretical thought for its time, considering that the collective burial rites were believed to have been established by none other than Maat, the goddess of divine justice. Here, very early in the history of civilization, we have an example of a differentiation between an institutionalized moral code and individual conscience.

Also to be thought of in this context was Socrates and his *daimonion*, an expression of his personal conscience. All founders of religious movements, moreover, have stood in notably close contact with their own consciences. Virtually all the great medieval mystics who later became saints were regarded by official doctrine as heretics at one time or another. From Luther to Solzhenitsyn or Sakharov, outstanding figures have defended their personal conscience with great courage against the official value

[8]H. Jacobsohn "The Dialogue of a World-Weary Man with His Ba," in *Timeless Documents of the Soul* (part of the series "Studies from the C. G. Jung Institute, Zurich"). Evanston, Illinois: Northwestern University Press, 1968.

structures, demonstrating the kind of strength of conscience which often characterizes cultural heroes.

For ordinary mortals, however, another question arises with regard to human conscience. We have already observed that, in the form of "concern"—worry over the threatened loss of harmony with the loved one or with a higher order—conscience is an important regulator both for the behavior of the individual in his social setting and for the social group itself. Does it not thus merge with the prevalent behavioral code of a society, which is internalized via the media of parents, family and schooling and then experienced as one's own conscience? And is this tendency to amalgamate with the prevalent value structures not further accentuated because infantile "concern" is linked to fear of isolation, encouraging the individual to identify himself with the collective code of behavior in order to avoid loss of love?

Indeed, "concern" understood as "compassion" or "caring" has consequences on two levels. For one thing every society is dependent on the sense of responsibility of a majority of its members. Concerned compassion is of decisive importance for mature communication between human beings and is therefore highly regarded as a virtue closely linked to conscience. At the same time, as we have already seen, "concern" is not purely altruistic, since it is also based on the fear of isolation and loss of love. This is why the need for responsible and conscientious behavior is vital for the welfare of the individual as well.

On the one hand, the effectiveness of every virtue is more reliable when it is based on more than just idealistic altruism. "Pure altruism" as an ethical imperative is an illusion. In the rare cases in which it seems to be in evidence, on closer examination it generally turns out to be connected to a masochistic need for self-sacrifice. The Christian commandment is "Love thy neighbor *as* thyself," not "*more than* thyself." In my opinion, it is natural to derive a kind of personal satisfaction, a very basic and legitimate inner gratification, from one's own conscientious behavior.

On the other hand, the reliability of the concern-based functions of conscience is problematical precisely because they are coupled with the fear of isolation and loss of love. The unconscious coupling of conscience with that fear is surely in some measure responsible for the fact that an individual's personal moral sense can be so easily lost in group or mass conscience. At such a time the views and values of the group to which one belongs are willingly accepted and replace one's own inner value judgments and decision-making potential.

All of this can take place more or less unconsciously, controlled by the fear of isolation and loss of love latent within us all. Identification with group ideals can also provide an easy way out of taking responsibility for individual decisions. What is most frequently to be observed, however, is that an internalized social value system replaces an individual's innermost voice of conscience. Then "good" or "evil" are perceived as whatever the collective says they are.

In an individual, the replacement of the personal moral sense through imprinting of the social group's moral code may have its root in the fact that, in infancy, the individual may not have sufficiently experienced and integrated the mother's empathic caring for his own inner reality. The young child's "concern," its worry about not destroying the mother and thus the foundations of its own existence, may then result in excessively early adjustment to the expectations of the world around it. A great many children never experience an almost unconditional attention to and caring for their total being, but only conditional love. The conditions generally amount to: If you will be as Daddy and Mommy want you to be, then we will love you.

Every child must make an adjustment of this kind, of course. But it is important that it not be demanded too soon. First the early beginnings of the child's personal moral sense should be encouraged. And that encouragement is provided when loving acknowledgment is given to the child's specific nature, when its psychic spontaneity and growing autonomy are affirmed and supported in a manner appropriate to its age. With the child's increasing maturity, parental adjustment to its psychic needs should be mixed with educative demands to a balanced degree which promotes and supports the child's own efforts at adjustment.

In this way the foundation is laid for a development in which the demands and values of a particular moral code are to a certain extent intertwined with the child's own personal moral sense. The personal call from the "voice of the God of Paradise"—i.e.,

creative inner knowledge linked to the totality of human nature—
is then brought into a developmentally appropriate connection
with the normative authority of the father archetype and its socio-
cultural context.

In the case of parental attention involving *conditional* love, the
conditions are generally inappropriate to the child's maturity and
frequently serve the parents' own needs. The child is forced to adjust in order to survive emotionally, which is tantamount to early
self-alienation. The same effect is created when the conditions imposed on the child's behavior change frequently on parental
whim, or when the conditions set by one parent are in conflict
with those of the other. Such a situation may be the root of later
opportunism, conscious or unconscious, in which adjustment to
the expectations of the momentary environment has become an
internalized axiom.

An individual who has developed in this way feels no confidence in anything that manifests itself through an inner voice,
places no value on his own internal standards. As a consequence
the concept of Paradise, the desire for conflict-free harmony, is
projected into the wish to be at one with the human environment,
to "howl with the wolves and run with the hounds," to act
collectively.

Commonly held beliefs and values are then unquestioningly accepted as personal values. And so it is that the personal moral
sense, personal conscience, may be dissolved and swept along in
a mass movement whose moral code may be extremely dubious.
C. G. Jung was always greatly concerned about the dangers of the
"mass psyche." He wrote ". . . as we all know, things are never
so bad when everybody is in the same boat. No doubts can exist in the herd; the bigger the crowd the better the truth—and the
greater the catastrophe."[9]

Man's ethical function, then, is anything but reliable; even with
the best intentions, it can all too easily be perverted. It is remarkable that mankind's most gruesome acts, wars of aggression,
terrorism, genocide, etc., are accompanied by justifications and
committed in the name of some alleged "supreme value," of a
divinity or a "God-given" idea ("For God, Emperor and Coun-

[9]C. G. Jung,*Collected Works* Vol. 12, p. 481.

try"). In our own day it is generally in the name of some *ism* or of a "supreme value" commonly termed Revolution.

In addition to all the varieties of physical force available for the suppression of any resistance, totalitarian states usually make massive efforts to influence the conscience of the people. To that end, distortions of fact and crass falsehoods are the order of the day. (Such intensive efforts, of course, only prove that the factor of conscience must always be taken into account.) Ideological rationalizations are served up in order to win unqualified agreement, to harmonize the conscience of the individual with the intentions of the rulers.

A frequently used ethical justification (i.e., a common method of pacifying conscience) is the assertion that supremely desirable ends justify any and all means. The perverted moral codes of such ideologies often exert a strong attraction. Resistance against their seductive power arises out of the individual's relation to the "God of Paradise," the voice of his own totality as a human being. This was Jung's opinion as well, as indicated by these words written in 1918, just after World War I:

> Individual self-reflection, return of the individual to the ground of human nature, to his own deepest being with its individual and social destiny—here is the beginning of a cure for that blindness which reigns at the present hour.[10]

[10]*Collected Works*, Vol. 7, p. 5

11. Original Sin and the Problem of the Shadow

There is a component of shadow in every expression of our lives—a fact which makes the idea of original sin quite comprehensible. It was Jung who first chose the word *shadow* to serve as a specialized psychological term. He understood it as representing those characteristics and tendencies in the personality which the conscious ego is unwilling or unable to acknowledge and accept as part of itself. For the most part these are the dark impulses in ourselves, to which Goethe referred as the "earthly remnant, painful to bear."

As Jung rightfully observed: "The living form needs deep shadow if it is to appear plastic. Without shadow it remains a two-dimensional phantom."[1] It seems to me that Jung's choice of the term "shadow" is a most felicitous one. In nature, shadow is created by light; where there is light, there is shadow as well. Light is also the symbol for the brightness of consciousness—which makes it graphically clear that illumination by consciousness always casts a shadow at the same time. Thus the specific form, content and effect of the shadow is largely determined by those value-attitudes with which the ego identifies itself.

Another reason why I find the choice of the term shadow appropriate is because we generally understand the idea of "the dark" to include not only that which is morally inferior but also things unclear, unilluminated, still unconscious. And so we cannot simply equate shadow with that which is absolutely negative

[1]Jung, *Collected Works*, Vol. 7, pp. 238–239.

or evil. It is only the "negative" of the image which we make of ourselves. And that image is closely linked to the experiences of early childhood, to our upbringing and our collective values, all of which greatly determine our personal development.

Jung writes:

> If the repressed tendencies, the shadow as I call them, were obviously evil, there would be no problem whatever. But the shadow is merely somewhat inferior, primitive, unadapted, and awkward; not wholly bad. It even contains childish or primitive qualities which would in a way vitalize and embellish human existence, but—convention forbids![2]

The shadow, then, is the "so-called evil" in a given situation; but, as depth psychology has discovered, it can have extremely destructive effects, primarily through splitting off from the conscious, responsible personality. "Everyone carries a shadow, and the less it is embodied in the individual's conscious life, the blacker and denser it is."[3]

The discovery of the enormous danger of the shadow in its repressed, submerged, split-off form provided depth psychology with the impetus to found a "new ethic."[4] Its main objective is the acknowledgment, elevation to consciousness, and assimilation of all those tendencies within us which we normally prefer to ignore because they subject our sense of self-esteem to an often severe test. Frequently there is virtually insurmountable resistance to this goal. That is one reason why, even today, every form of psychoanalysis still meets with emphatic rejection among broad segments of the populace.

Freudian analysis had to struggle long and hard before it gained some degree of acceptance; it was widely thought to be concerned only with "filth" and the "swamps of the mind" (which admittedly might be regarded as unedifying). It should be remarked here that, although the Freudian variety of psychoanalysis does not make use of the term "shadow," it strives to elevate unconscious contents into consciousness and thus to extend the

[2]*Collected Works*, Vol. 11, p. 78.
[3]Ibid., p. 76.
[4]Erich Neumann, *Depth Psychology and a New Ethic*. New York: G. P. Putnam's Sons, for the C. G. Jung Foundation, 1969.

ego's control over the dark, instinctual realm of the psyche, the "black tide of mud" which is the id.

The danger of shadow contents, as long as they are repressed or split off from consciousness, stems in part from the fact that they generally manifest themselves as projections onto other people. Traits and tendencies which we unconsciously reject in ourselves irritate us terribly in people around us. Feelings of hatred are thus generated, which often serve to mask a certain degree of envy. We envy a person who has the courage or the psychic constitution to live out aspects of the personality which we ourselves feel compelled to reject or repress because of our internalized ego-ideals and values.

An honest housewife, for example, who compulsively drives herself from morning till evening to keep her home spotlessly clean, may hate the woman next door who permits herself the freedom to sit in her garden and read a book in broad daylight or not to get up at dawn each day. The housewife feels constrained to repress such "laxity" in herself and so she hates her neighbor, harasses her and feels morally justified in doing so. She sees herself as good, industrious, embodying high moral values, while the woman next door is bad, objectionable. In reality, of course, her neighbor has done her absolutely no harm; it is quite enough that the other woman acts out aspects of life which the housewife must repress in herself.

Most hostility is based on such processes, by which other people are made to carry the projections of our own shadows. The all too familiar social and psychological consequences include the grisly persecution of racial and religious minorities. Similarly, countless interpersonal problems derive from such projective mechanisms, and are as harmful to our own psychic health as to the objects of our animosities. I should like to cite two examples from my therapy practice.

A young violinist came to see me, suffering from extreme stage fright. Before each public appearance she was overcome by such anxiety that she would take an overdose of tranquilizer, with the result that she seemed almost somnolent on stage. The trait that struck me most during her first visit to my office was an inclination to bubbly chatter, consisting of an odd mixture of childishly original thoughts and embarrassing clichés. The impression this created was of a girl in whom an impetuous temperament demanded expression, but who at the same time always felt impelled to prove herself the well-bred daughter of a good family and therefore constantly to apologize for her wild nature. Such a need for apology and reparation creates considerable difficulty on stage. During a performance there is only the music (or dance, drama, etc.), but no possibility for apology or subsequent restitution.

It was clear from the outset that this young woman somehow could not accept her own wild temperament. Soon afterward she dreamed that an acquaintance of hers, whom she actually hated, constantly lay in wait for her, plagued her and tried to beat her up. The dreamer proposed to call the police and have her acquaintance put away as a lunatic. At this point the other young woman asked to speak with the dreamer and told her that she was forced to persecute her only because she was jealous of her family. With that the dream ended.

When I asked the violinist why she hated that woman in reality, she replied: "Well, you see, she gets on my nerves horribly, because she has such loose relationships with men. She's a singer, but she is so ice-cold that she never suffers from stage fright." Our violinist secretly envied the other woman, then, for her sexual freedom and generally easy way of life, something which she was unable to permit herself. She had a male friend, but fended off his efforts at physical intimacy, insisting that she wanted to be pure when she got married, as her parents had been. Hence she was forced to suppress her own sexual impulses, although she was plagued by them. Those impulses were to be "put away"—i.e., repressed—by her internal keepers of law and order, symbolized by the police in her dream. But the price for such rigid imprisonment was hatred and a paralyzing case of stage fright.

It is interesting to note that the singer of whom she dreamed was not only more "liberated" sexually, but also apparently untroubled by stage fright. No one can really make music when they are constantly concerned about suppressing a side of themselves which they regard as unacceptable. Complete dedication to the music is thus made impossible, for musical expression requires the full vitality of the whole person. Behind the violinist's symptom of stage fright there was evidently a conflict with her own vitality and a good deal of repressed sexuality, all of which was symbolized in a "shadow figure."

Before dealing with the consequences of this discovery, let us briefly examine a second case. It involves a young man who had a vast anger against the "establishment." His aggressivity brought him into repeated difficulty and he suffered from not gaining the recognition he felt he deserved. He saw himself as too much a lover of truth, with too much integrity to be successful in this society, since all success requires a person to prostitute himself. As a result he hated everyone who was in any way successful. In a dream he encountered a successful person whom, in reality, he hated above all others. This successful man showed an interest in the dreamer, however, and tried to become his friend, whereupon the dreamer felt himself flattered and eagerly accepted the proffered friendship.

The successful man in his dream embodied the dreamer's own vast ambition, his longing to be recognized by society and to play a significant role in it. But such a drive for prestige does not fit the ego-ideal of a "man of integrity" who regards all striving for success as prostitution and thus as "shadowy." The repression of his need for prestige had its price, however: hatred. He himself termed his feelings of hatred "justified anger," although his attitude repeatedly angered others and sabotaged his own inner need for love, admiration and recognition.

In these two instances we see that bringing connections and motivations into consciousness creates a new moral problem. In the first case, the "ideal of purity" taken over from the parents causes suppression and repression of a significant portion of the individual's natural vitality; the results are feelings of hatred and a limitation of professional competence because of a paralyzing degree of stage fright.

In the second instance, the young man clings to the ideal of uncompromising personal "integrity" and thus represses his own intense need for status; the results are severe feelings of aggression toward the outside world and impairment of his own personal and professional prospects.

In both cases, it seems to me, the baby is being thrown out with the bathwater. The consequences of a moral position turn out to be extremely questionable, while the individual's own repressed drives are projected onto other people in the environment and rejected, with self-damaging effects.

It is noteworthy that both dreams we have described not only reveal the inner conflict but also point to a resolution. In both cases the dreams involve closer contact with a hated opponent. This means, first of all, a confrontation with the feelings of hatred and rejection triggered in the dreamer by that other person. The questions raised are: Why do I so rigorously reject my own sexual impulses, my own ambitions? They are still with me, even though I try not to admit them, and through projections they cause trouble for others and ultimately for myself as well. What values are at work within me, causing me to condemn as evil such essentially natural drives?

Such questions must be raised in contacting and confronting the rejected parts of the personality, in order to avoid the kind of unconscious immorality often caused by a rigorously "moral" conscious attitude. But this does not mean that our young violinist must necessarily undertake promiscuous relations with men as her hated singer-acquaintance does, or that the young man must become a career-hungry opportunist. The objective is not to "fall into" the shadow, but to develop a certain tolerance toward oneself, including all those aspects of the personality which do not fit one's own ego-ideals. This makes possible what is known as "withdrawing the projection," which in turn is a prerequisite for greater tolerance toward others.

The young woman violinist, in withdrawing her projections on others, came to see how little a sense of responsibility for herself she had developed up to that point in her life, having simply taken over her parents' values. She also realized that she had remained stuck in such childish dependence on her parents because she was afraid of the demands which life makes on a mature, adult woman. Her veil of moral rectitude had served not only to protect her against her own instinctual drives but also to mask her fear of responsibility for her own decisions. As she gained these insights she became less rigid toward her male friend and her stage fright declined to a normal level at which it no longer was an obstacle to her concert career.

As to our angry young man, he finally had to admit that the need to succeed was very active within him and that he wanted nothing so much as to become one of those successful people he had so vehemently condemned. He was forced to take a conscious attitude toward his own ambition, so that he could harness it responsibly for constructive ends. This made him more tolerant toward others and toward himself—certainly a gain in moral stature.

Negatively judged aspects of the personality are thus not to be suppressed or repressed, but rather drawn into the realm of responsible consciousness, which admittedly is often a much more difficult undertaking. But experience repeatedly shows that openness toward those sides of one's own personality that are felt to be inferior or immoral can provide the impetus for valuable changes in attitude, greater maturity and a heightened sense of responsibility.

In their profound wisdom, many fairytales make the same observation in their own fashion.[5] In the Grimm tale of "The Frog-King," the loathsome frog must be invited to table, taken to bed, actually grabbed by the princess and flung against the wall— and only then is the unappetizing beast transformed into a handsome prince. In "The Devil With the Three Golden Hairs," it is the despised Devil who has the wisdom to know why the world has become so sterile. Here the Devil signifies a side in ourselves which we unconsciously "demonize" and which we then despise in others. Thus fairytales, too, may be seen to speak of contacting and confronting the shadow, just as did the two dreams cited earlier.

The shadow is there, whether we wish to take account of it or not. It is inherent in all humans and serves to bring the ego back down to earth when it threatens to float off in an inflation. Knowledge of the shadow's existence helps counteract illusory blind faith in "progress," both with respect to humanity in general and ourselves in particular. From the standpoint of some "absolute good," everything we do is questionable and tinged with shadow. There is the example of modern medicine, which has made enormous progress and aims at something ethically unassailable, the healing of the individual and the prolongation

[5]See, for example, M. Jacoby, "Märcheninterpretation aus der Sicht C. G. Jungs" in M. Jacoby, V. Kast, and I. Riedel, *Das Böse im Märchen* (Evil in Fairytales). Fellbach: Bonz, 1978.

of human life. But as welcome as it is, medical progress has its shadow side, of which the so-called population explosion is just one example. Another is the fact that many hospitals and psychiatric clinics are full-to-bursting with old, senile or arteriosclerotic people who are kept alive with medication although their psychic life has essentially ceased. This is not a plea for euthanasia; we cannot arrogate to ourselves the right to decide which life is worth maintaining and which is not. But we are confronted with the fact that our very laudable medical progress is at the same time highly problematical and casts its own shadow. So it behooves us to include knowledge of the shadow side in every decision; otherwise we fall prey to utopian illusions and project our own shadows onto those people who do not share the same illusions.

Such projection occurs whenever there is missionary zeal for a cause or an idea which is regarded as ideal or absolutely good. For example, the concept of a perfectly just social order is something essentially positive, certainly worth striving for. But when it is overvalued, when any and all means are deemed justified to achieve that aim, perhaps via "revolution," then what becomes split off from consciousness is the realization that there has never been a society providing optimal justice for every individual, that because of its complexity all human social organization has a shadow component. Those who do not share the illusion that the new social order will be perfectly just are labeled "reactionaries" who stand in the way of its realization and thus become the new carriers of shadow projections.

Identification with a utopian faith requires that every semblance of doubt be uprooted, stamped out in oneself and in others. All means to achieve that end, from defamation to brute force, are deemed "just." This is not to say that current criticism of our society is entirely unjustified. Often it is right on the mark and provides valuable stimulation for further thought. But those who are criticized tend to be made insecure by such "attacks," and thus see only the shadow aspect of all the incorrigible utopians and dangerous revolutionaries. The shadow unconsciously contaminates both sides of the issue, unfortunately, turning differences of opinion into schematic hostility and making aggression appear justified.

At the same time, the knowledge that everything we do is tinged with shadow does not mean that we must simply fold our hands and cease striving for any sort of progress. There is always the danger that this knowledge may paralyze initiative and lead to a kind of pseudo-wise fatalism; it might be thought that no effort for improvement is sensible, since it is all contaminated by shadow. The response may be found in Goethe, whose writings seem to contain an appropriate quote for nearly any situation: *"Gestaltung, Umgestaltung, des ewigen Sinnes ewige Unterhaltung"* ("Creation, transformation, eternal mind's eternal recreation"). That is to say, creation and change are a psychic necessity of our human existence. Were we actually able to get rid of the shadow once and for all, there would be no more impulse to create, to improve and change.

Seen from that more profound perspective, the shadow is "part of that power which would always do evil yet always creates good," as Goethe phrases it in *Faust*. Setbacks, obstacles and disappointments in ourselves and others are not usually in keeping with our conscious desires; quite the contrary. But they often force us to reorient ourselves, sometimes providing the inner impetus for a creative transformation of our lives. Without "shadow" we would exist in paradisial perfection and would have no need to strive, create or change anything in this world.

It is, then, always worth keeping in mind that, in psychological terms, *original sin* comes very close to what we understand by *shadow*. Jung seems to have had a similar idea in mind when he wrote:

> We know of course that without sin there is no repentance and without repentance no redeeming grace, also that without original sin the redemption of the world could never have come about; but we assiduously avoid investigating whether in this very power of evil God might not have placed some special purpose which it is most important for us to know. One often feels driven to some such view when, like the psychotherapist, one has to deal with people who are confronted with their blackest shadow.[6]

Hence, when I unquestioningly fight against, suppress or repress that which I perceive as evil, I neglect the fundamentally human function of inquiry. I fail to ask what meaning or purpose might be contained in that so-called evil. I do not look it squarely in the eye, in order to assimilate it into my orientation toward

[6]Jung, *Collected Works*, Vol. 12, pp. 29–30.

myself and the world. Therefore I remain insufficiently aware of what I am doing. Sometimes, as a result, I unconsciously do evil in the name of doing good. I love my neighbor and do not notice how my undue concern tyrannizes him. I speak the unvarnished truth to people around me and remain oblivious to the subjectivity of that "truth" and to my own arrogant tactlessness and lack of understanding for the experience of others. With the best intentions I am helpful to others, but I fail to observe how much I thereby want to make them gratefully dependent upon me in order to increase my own self-esteem. I fight for a just society, and since I am convinced that what I am fighting for is "good" I am prepared to employ any means to achieve that end.

The shadow is always present, even with the best intentions, and it is extremely important to admit that fact to oneself. The contents of the shadow are part of the variegated kaleidoscope of human behavior and imagination. It is perfectly human to have incestuous wishes, perverse fantasies, utopian dreams, overweening ambitions, aggressive death-wishes against those who stand in our way. One need not be ashamed of such things in oneself and try to repress them, since they are part of being human. They often rise into consciousness unbidden, autonomously. When we find the courage to look them in the eye and inquire as to their sense and meaning, they often take on a different valence. Their meaning is most likely to become clear when we try to understand them not only concretely but also symbolically. Then it frequently turns out that they symbolize inner tendencies toward self-realization.

To take just one example: The fantasy of wishing to kill my father, the familiar Oedipus motif, may be telling me symbolically that it is high time I move beyond the constraints of paternal authority and the value norms which I have unconsciously taken over from it, in order for me to become truly adult and to assume full responsibility for my own existence. The death of the father in a dream, though often interpreted as the dreamer's death-wish toward his or her actual father, ultimately points to the same basic theme of assuming responsibility for one's own life.

In any case, it is possible to develop a new attitude toward our most ignoble fantasies and to draw them into the circle of our conscious sense of responsibility. This makes us aware of the variety and profundity of human existence. In this way we also feel ourselves to be more human in the fullest sense of the term and less concerned about always saving face. When I come to know my own shadow, to include it in my conscious attitude, I am no longer so susceptible to the judgment of others around me, less bothered by the fear of being seen through and thus devalued.

It is not difficult to realize how much such a shift in attitude can also ease tensions in the realm of interpersonal relations. A father who is open to the realization of how his own shadow operates within him no longer demands his children's blind obedience and respect for his authority solely because these things are due him as the father. In other words, he need not be constantly concerned with acknowledgment of his paternal dignity and feel himself aggrieved each time his authority is questioned. Either he possesses a natural authority by virtue of his personal maturity and strength, and therefore does not fear admitting mistakes, or his presumed authority rests on a very shaky base.

There is no denying that the shadow inherent in everything human creates immeasurable problems. An avoidance of these problems leads to neurotic constriction or to projection of the shadow onto the outside world and resulting blindness. Acceptance of one's own shadow is often very painful and requires great moral courage. The benefits it brings are greater tolerance, modesty, genuineness and an enrichment of psychic dimensions. In addition there is an increased differentiation of judgment, thanks to which simplistic black and white are seen to be merely two facets of an almost endless spectrum. The life of the psyche is profoundly diverse.

In dealing with the shadow problem, which calls our entire value hierarchy into question, we need to keep Jung's warning in mind:

> It is of course a fundamental mistake to imagine that when we see the non-value in a value or the untruth in a truth, the value or the truth ceases to exist. It has only become *relative*. Everything human is relative, because everything rests on an inner polarity, for everything is a phenomenon of energy. Energy necessarily depends on a pre-existing polarity, without which there could be no energy . . . Therefore the tendency to deny all previous values in favour of their opposites is just as much of an exaggeration as

the earlier one-sidedness. And insofar as it is a question of rejecting universally accepted and indubitable values, the result is a fatal
loss. One who acts in this way empties himself out with his
values.[7]

As soon as we expose ourselves to the reality of the shadow and
propose making it conscious and acknowledging it, the question
of conscience becomes highly complex. We no longer know what
we can guide ourselves by, since the moral code which we have
introjected as the superego has been called into question. This
moral code tries to distribute light and shadow and to draw clear
lines of demarcation between them. But in the process yet another
bit of shadow easily creeps in unnoticed, bearing the features of
false security, inflexibility, self-righteousness, hypocrisy. In many
cases this rigidity obstructs the individual's development toward
maturity and self-responsibility. In such a situation it may be of
critical importance for me to turn my awareness to that innermost
conscience which we have referred to as "the voice of the God
of Paradise." This is the voice of the principle of natural creativity,
which calls out: "Adam, where are you?"—that is, have you hidden yourself, lost your way, blocked the path to your own sense
of wholeness? And in posing these questions, it sets the "measure
of the human."

[7]*Collected Works*, Vol. 7, p. 75.

12. Jung's "Collision of Duties"

Jung recognized the effectiveness of conscience in the symbol of the *vox Dei*, the voice of God. In his essay "A Psychological View of Conscience,"[1] he differentiates between a "moral" form of conscience and an "ethical" form. The moral form is based on mores, generally accepted customs, while in the case of ethical acts of conscience, "Only the creative power of the ethos that expresses the whole man can pronounce the final judgment."[2] This generally occurs "when two decisions or ways of acting, both affirmed to be moral and therefore regarded as 'duties,' collide with one another."[3] In a collision of duties, a judgment is called for which cannot really be termed moral.

> Here the decision has no custom at its disposal on which it could rely. The deciding factor . . . proceeds not from the traditional moral code but from the unconscious personality . . . If one is sufficiently conscientious the conflict is endured to the end, and a creative solution emerges which is produced by the constellated archetype and possesses that compelling authority not unjustly characterized as the voice of God. The nature of the solution is in accord with the deepest foundations of the personality as well as with its wholeness; it embraces conscious and unconscious and therefore transcends the ego.[4]

Let us examine a relatively banal example of the collision of duties from everyday life: Assume that a married man with

[1] *Collected Works*, Vol. 10, pp. 437–455.
[2] Ibid., p. 454.
[3] Ibid.
[4] Ibid., pp. 454–455.

children has taken his widowed mother into his house, in keeping with the Fourth Commandment, "Honor your father and your mother." As happens all too often, however, this creates a tense emotional atmosphere in the family, with the man's mother and wife getting along very badly. The younger woman feels herself patronized and watched over by her mother-in-law; she objects to her overly lenient (or alternatively, rigidly old-fashioned) influence on the children's upbringing. For her part, the mother-in-law feels it incumbent on her to be helpful, which answers to her own needs and may indeed also be expected of her. But whatever help she offers is rejected, criticized as interference. And that accusation, too, probably contains a kernel of truth, based on the older woman's unconscious desire to dominate. The mutual jealousy being played out in the shadows of these two women, the presence of an unconscious mother-complex, perhaps also a devilishly opinionated animus—in short, a whole arsenal of unconscious needs, fears and conflicts—lend a familiar, overly emotional intensity to this commonplace drama.

What is to happen now? Would it not be better for the mother-in-law to move to a home for the elderly? Today's code of behavior no longer takes the Fourth Commandment quite so literally; the "senior citizens' home" solution would not be looked at askance. But the man of the family feels stirrings of conscience. There is a collision of duties: On the one hand, his need to be a good husband and father and to heed the concerns of his wife and children; on the other hand, his desire to offer a home to his old, widowed mother.

Naturally, this man's own mother-complex, with its unconscious ties, desires and fears, colors his relations to both his mother and his wife. But even if, through analysis, he were to become conscious of the now-unconscious motivations behind his mother-wife dilemma, any decision he takes will mean accepting a certain burden of guilt. If he does nothing to alter the situation, he will make a mockery of his own insistence that he wants to do what is best for everyone; it would be self-deception, in view of the unbearable tensions afflicting all parties concerned. There is no "clean" solution to this problem; there is only "acting according to the best of my knowledge and conscience"—which is usually not good enough.

Perhaps this tension will provide the impetus necessary to find an interim solution which no one has thought of so far. Perhaps everyone involved will gain in maturity as a result of the conflict. Or perhaps the situation will remain nasty and destructive, poisoning the atmosphere and harming the children. Perhaps, for that reason, the old-age home is actually the only solution, along with the suffering and pangs of conscience it would bring. Again, perhaps the mother/mother-in-law will provide the point of crystallization which will bind this man and his wife closer together —or drive them apart.

In any case, no outsider can legitimately offer advice on this problem. The people involved must find their own "knowing," confront their own consciences. As a therapist one can assist in the decisionmaking process only by helping to increase sensitivity to various aspects of the conflict and to the inner voice of conscience.

As has already been mentioned, the need for a moral code is an archetypal part of mankind. It is symbolized by the image of the law-giving father god. The inner conscience, which Winnicott speaks of as moral sensibility and which develops naturally in early childhood when "the child's innate order accords with the order implemented by its mother,"[5] need not necessarily be perceived as the polar opposite of the moral code. The two components of conscience may interweave and supplement one another. The commandment issued by the father god lays down a principle: "Honor your father and your mother." How that principle is applied in a given case, however, is left up to the individual's "moral sensibility," which provides the attitude adequate to the particular situation.

The principle "You shall not bear false witness against your neighbor" is of extraordinary importance. Unless it is possible to have confidence in the word of honor of another person, human relations rest on a very weak foundation and social organization is corrupt. Untruth is a sin against one's own soul. But one's "moral sensibility" may relativize the principle. There are situations in which a certain measure of untruth may be more ethical. Here is an example:

[5]Neumann, *The Child*, p. 91.

Some years ago a young woman became an inpatient at a psychiatric clinic because of a severe neurosis. Subsequently the therapy was continued on an outpatient basis. She improved to the point where she registered for a training course at a trade school, a sensible step with a view to future employment. The head of the school requested a letter of recommendation from the woman's therapist. In writing the letter, the therapist deliberately omitted any mention of the woman's earlier stay in a clinic. The woman was accepted for training.

A year later the school director learned in a roundabout manner of her period as an inpatient at a psychiatric clinic. He telephoned the therapist and angrily accused him of providing false information. The therapist asked: "How is she doing in school?" The reply: "No complaints on that score, except for her extreme shyness." To which the therapist said: "I deliberately withheld the information about her stay at the clinic. Tell me truthfully: If I had told you everything, are you certain that you would have approved her application anyway?" The head of the school, an honest man, had no answer to that question.

The story speaks for itself. Obviously, to the therapist's moral sensibility the chance for this woman to receive quality training for her future was of greater importance than the requirement of absolute truthfulness. As it turned out, his caution was justified, although one would expect the head of a school to show understanding in such a matter.

More clearly than in such everyday situations, however, conscience as the *vox Dei*, the voice of God, is to be heard in more difficult borderline situations, such as under political conditions where following one's own conscience may bring severe sanctions in its wake. Understandably enough, it is not given to large numbers of people to accept the possibility of martyrdom out of loyalty to their conscience.

In the final analysis, experience shows there is no gainsaying Jung's observation:

> Besides the "right" kind of conscience there is a "wrong" one, which exaggerates, perverts, and twists evil into good and good into evil just as our own scruples do; and it does so with the same compulsiveness and with the same emotional consequences as the

"right" kind of conscience. Were it not for this paradox the question of conscience would present no problem; we could then rely wholly on its decisions so far as morality is concerned. But since there is great and justified uncertainty in this regard, it needs unusual courage or—what amounts to the same thing—unshakable faith for a person simply to follow the dictates of his own conscience.[6]

As Jung also points out: "There is scarcely any other psychic phenomenon that shows the polarity of the psyche in a clearer light than conscience."[7] Polarity is an essential structural element in the human psyche, and conscience brings the "ever-present and necessary opposites to conscious perception." Jung goes on to conclude: ". . . if the *vox Dei* conception of conscience is correct, we are faced logically with a metaphysical dilemma: either there is a dualism, and God's omnipotence is halved, or the opposites are contained in the monotheistic God-image, as for instance in the Old Testament image of Yahweh, which shows us morally contradictory opposites existing side by side."[8]

It should again be stressed here that, in psychological terms, what is under discussion is always the *image* of God in the human psyche, and not "the Deity itself." Antinomies, moral ambivalence and paradox cannot be eliminated from that God-image.

[6]*Collected Works*, Vol. 10, p. 442.
[7]Ibid., p. 447.
[8]Ibid., pp. 447–448.

13. The Forbidden

It was the omnipotent, omniscient Lord of Creation himself who placed the serpent in Adam's Paradise. As has already been indicated, countless symbolic meanings are linked to the image of the serpent, which for mankind almost always has a sinister or uncanny quality. The snake lives in secret places; it is swift and sly in its hunting. With the casting of its skin it demonstrates a capacity for transformation and development, in the sense that it doffs its old covering, that which is dead, brittle, obsolete. The phallus-like shape of its head has often been associated with virility, masculine creativeness. But by its ability to spew poison and cause death the serpent can also symbolize the impulse to cold-blooded destruction. It represents, in any case, the experience of a dark, instinctual drive for change and transformation, an impulse which insures that life does not stand still—not even in Paradise.

Mankind has an instinctual need to alter the status quo, to throw off dependence and attain autonomous power. As C. Meves so rightly observes: "In every three- or four-year-old boy who stamps his foot and rebels against his parents' commands, or who tries to do in secret what he has been strictly forbidden to do, there lives the spirit of the serpent, the impulse to change, to throw off the shackles of dependence."[1] In any event our mythic report of Creation indicates that the development of consciousness is to be seen as an instinctual life principle, a natural drive in humankind.

[1] C. Meves, *Austreibung als Anstoss zur Reife* (Expulsion as the Impulse to Maturity), in J. Illies, *Die Sache mit dem Apfel* (The Business with the Apple), p. 58.

For all that, the biblical tale does not paint a very promising picture of human reality after the loss of Paradise. Enmity is established between woman and serpent, and between their descendants: ". . . he shall bruise your head, and you shall bruise his heel." Woman is henceforward to bring forth children in pain; man is to eat his bread in the sweat of his brow, for the earth is cursed because of him and shall bring forth thorns and thistles. And most important: "You are dust, and to dust you shall return." That is, death appears on the scene.

This is how the concrete terms of human existence are depicted in the Old Testament. The conditions of human life are perceived as a punishment. This is doubtless a theodicy, that is, a defense of the Lord of Creation's goodness despite the blatant questionableness of the situation in which his creatures find themselves. Everything good is seen as coming from God, while mankind has only itself to blame for all evil—a theological position which Jung vehemently attacked in his book "Answer to Job."²

²*Collected Works*, Vol. 11, pp. 355ff.

14. Suffering After the Fall

In considering the curse which immediately follows the acquisition of consciousness, we see that the first form of suffering it entails is the hostility between woman and her descendants and the serpent and its offspring. In the light of what has been said so far about the significance of the serpent, this might appear paradoxical at first. In terms of psychic reality, however, a certain vital energy inherent in the human species is invested in the development of consciousness; but as soon as a field of consciousness centered upon the ego has been developed, the fundamental human conflict becomes increasingly important: that is, mankind's specifically human disunity with its own "nature."

Development of ego-consciousness brings with it increasing control over one's own drives and instinctual impulses. We have already observed that Adolf Portmann characterizes humankind as "free to decide," in contrast to other animal species which he terms "instinct-bound." To the extent that a person exists as a creature with free decisionmaking power within the confines of his field of consciousness, a human loses his instinct-bond. The development of consciousness means falling out of unitary existence. Suddenly there is "spirit and flesh," and though the spirit may be willing the flesh is weak—or sometimes vice versa.

Irrespective of all differences between various individuals, groups and philosophies, irrespective even of the level of development of human economy, society and culture, man must be characterized as a needy creature of reason or a reasonable creature of needs.[1]

Thus the constant possibility of conflict is given, conflict with oneself as well as with one's fellow humans, where collisions of needs easily come about, with "reason" as a handy tool for providing the ways, means and justification for killing other humans with a clear conscience. Humanity has lost the instinctive inhibition against killing members of one's own species, an inhibition common to all other dangerous predators. Hence consciousness means assuming responsibility for one's own actions, with the constant struggle to keep the instinctual side in line, under control. In other words, the serpent is brought low: "Upon your belly shall you go."

But man cannot completely conquer the serpent. Hidden in the dust, it will always try to attack human weakness, the Achilles' heel. Aside from the fact that man and snake live in a state of mutual war in external reality, then, this enmity and disunity symbolize an anthropological fact. Primitive peoples have always used painful initiation rites to separate themselves from the power of instinct. In a later phase of development, ethics provide principles by means of which man's "serpent nature" is to be held in check. Psychotherapy must often concern itself with the bite in the heel, the painful symptoms with which the serpent wreaks vengeance for its repression and humiliation.

The second condition of suffering, pain in childbearing, should be bracketed with the last one, "You are dust, and to dust you shall return." It must be kept in mind here that Eve gave birth to nothing at all during her time in Paradise. Although death is threatened earlier as a consequence of violating the commandment, it is really only after the expulsion from Eden that birth and death actually appear on the scene. Here again, through the development of consciousness mankind is confronted with a basic condition of life: That is, life needs constant renewal, unceasing regeneration. And so, in nature there is a continual cycle of birth and death and individual creatures are its victims.

[1] O. Höffe, "Herrschaftsfreiheit oder gerechte Herrschaft?" (Arbitrary Rule or a Just Rule?), in *Neue Zürcher Zeitung*, section "Zeitfragen" (Issues of the Day), July 30–31, 1977.

Mankind, too, is ineluctably embedded in this natural cycle. But it is humanity's specifically human burden to live under this condition not in ignorance but in awareness. Man's life is stressed with the knowledge of decay and death. Consciousness of temporal limits also imposes bounds on man's fantasies of omnipotence. Death is the ever-present factor of risk and uncertainty in human life. The awareness of death is one of the most far-reaching sources of suffering in the mind of man.

As to the pain of childbirth, modern medicine is quite capable of obviating most of that pain by means of anesthesia. But many women reject such measures; they prefer to remain conscious, in order not to be deprived of so profound an experience no matter how painful it may be. If we also think of "giving birth" in an extended sense, as bearing spiritual or intellectual offspring, we know full well that there is generally a heavy price to pay for creativity, with innovation usually coming only after crisis. This is true for all social transformation, and the biographies of brilliantly creative individuals point in the same direction. It is a fact that may also be observed in everyday life, as well as in the practice of psychotherapy. New steps toward maturity are often accompanied by pain, which turns out to be the very thing that lends them lasting value.

Let us look at one more condition enumerated in the Genesis tale: "In the sweat of your face you shall eat bread." The philosophical anthropologist A. Gehlen has written: "In order to be able to exist, man is organized for the restructuring and conquering of nature. He is a creature of action, and his self-created culture becomes his environment."[2] Here we have reference to *homo faber*, man the maker, who by dint of his consciousness creates and reshapes.

In this context it is worth noting briefly how civilization, though essential and built by man's creative energy, becomes in time more and more of a burden to itself. The discontents of civilization are linked to man's profoundly divided nature, which has already been remarked upon. We are the beneficiaries, but also the victims, of *homo faber*'s enormous accomplishments. We

[2]A. Gehlen, *Der Mensch* (The Person), p. 35.

suffer from the compulsions imposed by our highly differentiated, modern culture with its vast technological potential.

The Nazis' efficient gas chambers as well as our world-threatening nuclear weapons are products of the creative capacity of *homo faber*, who has the ability to transform nature and the natural. The cancerous spread of technological civilization and its many side-effects has generated a large and much-discussed catalogue of problems, the details of which are familiar enough not to need any further elaboration here.

15. Consciousness and the Striving for "Bliss"

Obviously it is difficult to accept the conditions of human "reality." The young painter described earlier refused to acknowledge those conditions, and paid the price of an inner split and numerous psychosomatic symptoms. There was a strong drive in him to master existence, to give it meaning and to attain a measure of self-realization, but that drive came into conflict with his regressive fantasies of Paradise.

The widespread drug problem among young people today is also linked to an inability to accept the conflicted conditions of human existence. As Eberhard Jung writes: "The desire for Paradise is based on the misapprehension that there can be such a thing as problem-free life."[1] The same author makes some interesting remarks which support our premise that such a longing for Paradise involves a need to restore the infantile unitary reality.

> In this early phase the world of experience revolves around nourishment and skin-contact. Intensive perception through the various sense organs also plays an important role. The countless descriptions of drug experiences in which there is an intensification of sense perception along with a short-circuiting of consciousness and the awareness of time, are reminiscent of this early phase of human development. It is only as we develop a sense of time that we learn to bear the tension until the next gratification. There are strong indications that the effect of drugs is sought in

[1]Eberhard Jung, "Analytische Psychologie und Rauschmittelproblematik" (Analytical Psychology and Drug Problems), in *Zeitschrift für analytische Psychologie*, Vol. 6, No. 1, 1975, p. 20.

order to achieve a regression to this early phase of development, in which the pleasure principle is predominant.[2]

In an extended sense we may also speak of Paradise as a condition in which a person's "world design," i.e., his internal images and needs, are in complete harmony with external circumstances. Such a state is highly prized as "happiness." In reality, however, it is possible only for brief moments. And even these moments of happiness are often fully perceived as such only in retrospect. As Freud remarked:

> One feels inclined to say that the intention that man should be "happy" is not included in the plan of "Creation." What people call happiness in the strictest sense comes from the (preferably sudden) satisfaction of needs which have been dammed up to a high degree, and it is by its nature only possible as an episodic phenomenon. When any situation that is desired by the pleasure principle is prolonged, it only produces a feeling of mild contentment. We are so made that we can derive intense enjoyment only from a contrast and very little from a state of things. Thus our possibilities of happiness are already restricted by our constitution.[3]

There is often a strong desire to extend a situation in which inner expectations and images are in harmonious accord with external circumstance. But maintaining such a situation always requires at least a partial ignoring or reinterpreting of the facts to bring them into line with one's own "world design." This means that the critical factor of consciousness, the capacity to differentiate things from one another, is not applied where it really matters. Whenever a harmonious world is to be maintained, or to be achieved at some future date, the image of Paradise is always at work in the unconscious; one of the ways in which it invariably expresses itself is in the ignoring of certain aspects of human reality.

In the Genesis tale it is told how, after they had eaten of the fruit of the Tree of Knowledge, the eyes of Adam and Eve were opened. The paradisial state, that is, cannot be consciously perceived and realized as such. It can exist only so long as it is not

[2]Ibid., p. 21.
[3]Freud, *The Complete Psychological Works,* Vol. 21, p. 76.

consciously perceived or "known." This raises the question of whether "Paradise" might not also mean: I do not *see* how foul, thorny, naked and raw the conditions of existence really are. Only when my eyes are opened, like those of Adam and Eve, can I perceive reality—and as soon as that happens, paradisial existence is over, gone. Is it any wonder, then, that such stubborn resistance is frequently raised against increased consciousness? In the language of depth psychology, we speak of defense mechanisms such as denial and repression.

Therapeutic experience shows that the development of consciousness is the *conditio sine qua non* for healing and human maturity. But the Genesis tale appears to convey the opposite message: to wit, that consciousness brings guilt and suffering—a view which seems to be shared by many people who mount fierce resistance against expanding consciousness. And there may be some kernel of truth in the old saying, "What I don't know can't hurt me."

In this same context, some very serious questions of conscience frequently arise. For example, should a terminally ill person be told the truth under all circumstances, or may there be good reason to protect him from such knowledge? There is knowledge which may be more than a person can bear. In psychotherapy the therapist is repeatedly faced with the question of whether a patient is strong enough to handle certain confrontations, or whether the time has come yet for certain questions and interpretations. Jung wrote often about "legitimate resistances" which must be respected by the analyst.

On the whole, however, a positive attitude toward increased consciousness means encouraging the development of an integral ego, i.e., a person's ability to deal with both positive *and* negative experience in such a fashion that the integrity of the personality is maintained. To learn and accept the fact that the human state of being-in-conflict is actually necessary for the development of consciousness and maturity—this is the great lesson of "post-paradisial existence." As it is written: "Behold, the man has become like one of us, knowing good and evil."

The expansion of consciousness has always been regarded as a great positive value by the philosophers, beginning back in ancient Greece. "Know Thyself" was inscribed on the walls of

Apollo's shrine at Delphi. Socrates regarded himself as "a Philosopher, that is, an examiner of myself and of others" (Plato, *Apology*). And, as has been mentioned, all schools of analytical psychotherapy concentrate their efforts on expanding consciousness.

On this subject Jung has written:

> "But why on earth," you may ask, "should it be necessary for man to achieve, by hook or by crook, a higher level of consciousness?" This is truly the crucial question, and I do not find the answer easy. Instead of a real answer I can only make a confession of faith: I believe that, after thousands and millions of years, someone had to realize that this wonderful world of mountains and oceans, suns and moons, galaxies and nebulae, plants and animals, *exists*.[4]

According to Jung: "Without the reflecting consciousness of man the world is a gigantic meaningless machine, for as far as we know man is the only creature that can discover 'Meaning.'"[5]

But greater consciousness, and with it a far-reaching acceptance of the internal and external conditions of existence, is by no means synonymous with unqualified "adjustment" to any and all social circumstances. In fact a solidly grounded, well-developed consciousness has the best chance of seeing through those questionable and one-sided aspects of civilization which endanger the basic substance of humanity.

The idea of Paradise, however, remains operative in the human psyche in many ways. Among other things, it is expressed in the words "being happy." In part it may be equated with what A. Guggenbühl terms "well-being." He writes:

> Well-being has to do with the avoidance of unpleasant tensions, with striving for the possession of a physical sense of comfort, relaxed and pleasant. The state of well-being requires having sufficient nourishment, protection from the elements, an absence of anxiety about one's continuing existence, an easing of sexual tension now and then, and a pleasant though not exhausting amount of physical activity. Furthermore, it requires the possibility of satisfying some of the so-called material wishes without inordinate effort. Also a minimum of space for living is necessary. One should

[4]*Collected Works*, Vol. 9, I, p. 95.
[5]Aniela Jaffé, *The Myth of Meaning*. New York: published, by Putnam's for the C. G. Jung Foundation, 1971, p. 140.

not, however, understand well-being as purely physiological. A feeling of belonging to a group and enjoying a certain amount of prestige within one's collective group are necessary. Human security, a pleasant feeling of belonging to the herd, a good relationship within the family and among neighbors and relatives are indispensable.[6]

This definition brings us back to the concept of the good "environment mother" from the early stage of infancy.

Guggenbühl also enumerates those things which clearly do not belong to a state of well-being: ". . . tensions, dissatisfactions, painful emotions, anxiety, hatred, difficult and insoluble internal and external conflicts, obsessive searching for an undiscoverable truth, confused struggles about God, and the felt need to come to terms with evil and death."[7] Since people with a disturbed primal relationship experience sharp, often almost unbearable feelings of tension, conflict and dissatisfaction, the idea of Paradise exerts a concomitantly powerful attraction on them, frequently becoming the hook on which their vital energies are regressively hung. For them, the only consolation in this unbearable life is the fantasy of how things could be . . . *if*. (If only there were no such word as "if.")

The concept of Paradise need not be only passive and regressive in its effects, however. It may also have the character of a call, a challenge to improve things as they are. Since the earth is cursed (as the Bible tells us) to bear thorns and thistles, it has often failed to yield enough food despite all the "sweat of our brow." This situation still obtains today in the so-called developing countries. It was industrialization which gradually brought prosperity, security and the Lotus Land of the supermarket to large numbers of people. The machine, the foundation of industrialization, was and remains a magnificent product of man's inventive genius. But some of the consequences of industrialization were horrendous, with vast numbers of people, including children, being degraded to little more than labor slaves.

In today's Western democracies, despite numerous conflicts of interest, the struggle for distribution of national wealth has taken

[6]Adolf Guggenbühl-Craig, *Marriage—Dead or Alive*. Zurich: Spring Publications, 1977, p. 21.
[7]Ibid.

something of a new turn. The modern welfare state insures the distribution of wealth and income by means of progressive taxes. Some people laud such a system, others decry it. From the standpoint of social welfare, however, it provides a maximum number of people with an unprecedented level of material security.

The image of the Great Mother, caring, nurturing, swiftly cushioning life's basic risks, is thus projected upon the state. No one is to starve, go without medical care in case of illness, or be neglected in old age. This is good. The sensitivity to social issues, to justice and injustice, is now highly developed, especially among young people. But the welfare state as the "Good Mother" is frequently not "good enough" in meeting many needs. Time and again it is accused of neglect—and often rightly so.

It must be remembered, however, that in its role as the Great Nourishing Mother the state is not an immortal goddess with a never-failing source of nectar and ambrosia. Whether distributed more equitably or less, its gifts do not come from the inexhaustible primal ground of existence. The state is also the Devouring Mother, voracious even as she bares her nourishing breasts. The tribute paid to her is enormous, consisting of industrial overproduction and its attendant squandering of energy. This overproduction needs buyers, and so products are touted to the skies, by honest and dishonest means, to get them to the buying public. This is known as marketing.

And all of this demands an enormous expenditure of energy on the part of countless people, who collectively comprise our achievement-oriented society. The enticement to achieve is financial, the prospect of greater income, which in turn holds promise of a sense of happiness, greater well-being. The bait is the possibility of consuming more, greater narcissistic gratification, more prestige.

In their book, Parin and Morgenthaler[8] report on a Dogon village headman who, when asked why the white man seemed to be less happy than his own people, replied: "The whites think too much, and then they make many things, and the more they make the more they think. And then they earn much money, and when they have much money they worry that they might lose it and

---

[8]*Die Weissen denken zu viel* (White Men Think Too Much), p. 32.

have no more. So they think still more and make even more money and never have enough. And they know peace no more. This is why they are not happy." No commentary is needed on the keen observation and wisdom of this "primitive" person.

In any case, the state as Great Nourishing Mother needs money in order to make welfare possible. She takes it from her citizens. And when the citizens do not earn any money, of course, they are unable to give her any. It is perfectly fair for the wealthy to be called upon to give more than the less fortunate. But if too much is asked of them, they do not have enough left for new investments and structural improvements, with the result that production drops, there are fewer job openings and the Gross National Product declines. The rich too grow poorer, and Mother State grows hungrier.

Thus it is that our industrialized, achievement-oriented, consumer society produces the previously mentioned cancerous spread of technological civilization. Its symptoms are: the flood of concrete over natural land; landscapes of pollution-spewing factories; nuclear power plants; the rape of natural resources; ear-splitting noise from road traffic, pneumatic hammers, lawn mowers and the mechanization of agriculture.

In many respects all of this is of great importance for human "well-being," bringing an unprecedented increase in general living standards. But adjustment to the demands of high productivity and consumerism means an emphasis on achievement and competitiveness. To a tangible, indeed to a great degree, our earthly welfare paradise is a disappointment; the result is the upsurge of a compensatory longing for Paradise, since despite high living standards, supposed well-being and state welfare, the lived reality does not truly provide satisfaction.

It seems to me, though, that every age suffers from its own particular problems. Consequently, compensatory ideas of Paradise have always been, and remain, of considerable importance.

PART THREE

PARADISE: THE HOPE OF
FUTURE REDEMPTION

1. Paradise as Hope for the Future in Early Judaism and the New Testament

In the light of what has already been said, it is understandable that the idea of a future Paradise should have cropped up among the Jewish people during the period of political crisis before and during the Babylonian exile (587–538 B.C.). In that increasingly desperate situation the faithful hoped for help from the Lord God of Israel. Much of their hope centered on a surprising divine intervention in the political maneuvering of the great powers. The greater their suffering because of their own impotence and the scornful despotism of the enemy, the more emphatic became the expressions of belief in God's vengeance and in the ultimate victory.

It was in this troubled time that the voices of the Prophets were raised. Again and again they reminded the people of the special relationship between Israel and its God, fighting for purity of the faith in Yahweh against the polytheistic influences in the Canaanite and Babylonian territories, and most particularly against the cult of Baal. Among all the traditions of primeval beginnings, the Genesis tale of Paradise gained its special importance because the ideal primal condition which it described in the remote past was now also the hope for the future.

Deutero-Isaiah reports God as saying: "I will open rivers on the bare heights, and fountains in the midst of the valleys; I will make the wilderness a pool of water, and the dry land springs of water. I will put in the wilderness the cedar, the acacia, the myrtle, and the olive; I will set in the desert the cypress, the plane and the pine together; that men may see and know, may consider and under-stand together, that the hand of the Lord has done this, the Holy One of Israel has created it" (Isaiah 41:18–20).

And Ezekiel prophesied: "This land that was desolate has become like the garden of Eden; and the waste and desolate and ruined cities are now inhabited and fortified" (Ezekiel 36:35). In general there was an increasingly widespread fantasy that the crea-tion of primal times would be paralleled by a new creation at the end of days.

In the apocryphal Books of Enoch, Paradise is depicted as a place for the elect, the just, the saintly, situated at the extreme edge of heaven, the four rivers of Paradise flowing with honey, milk, oil and wine (Enoch 8:5). A notable element in this descrip-tion is that, as is often the case in apocalyptic literature, Paradise is here no longer regarded as an earthly spot but transferred to heaven. It is God's Garden, Land of the Blessed, a wondrous divine residence above the arch of heaven.

Hope of the happy primal time's return is also implicit in the idea that Jerusalem and Mount Zion will be transformed into the Garden of Paradise, with a mighty river flowing from holy Mount Zion in that future time—just as it did from the Paradise of Genesis. Here we encounter the concept of the Heavenly Jerusa-lem, which came to be of increasing importance. But the Messiah is needed for the fulfillment of this vision of the future, as is writ-ten in the Testament of Levi: "He himself [the Messiah] will open the gates of Paradise, will remove the sword which threatens Adam, will feed the saints from the Tree of Life, and the spirit of holiness will be upon them."[1]

Such ideas are not alien to the New Testament. Proclaiming the coming of God's Kingdom is, of course, an important element in Jesus' preaching. But it has departed from the concrete, political expectations of Judaism; it is "not of this world" (John 18:36). In Romans 14:17 there is the statement: "For the kingdom of God is not food and drink but righteousness and peace and joy in the Holy Spirit." And in Matthew 22:30 the point is made that "in the resurrection they neither marry nor are given in marriage, but are like angels in heaven."

[1] Cited under "Paradise" in H. Bächtold-Stäubli, *Handwörterbuch des deutschen Aberglaubens* (Handbook of German Superstition). Berlin & Leipzig: de Gruyter, 1927–1942.

In any case, the Christian concept of Paradise is not simply of something gone forever, from which mankind has been ejected. As the Kingdom of Heaven it is also the site of future eternal peace and the possibility of redemption, with the Gospels mentioning a number of indications given by Jesus of what the conditions might be for entering into that Kingdom. Here, too, the concept of Paradise means a vision of future participation in divine joy.[2]

[2]It is not possible within the confines of this work to deal with the flood of eschatological speculation in Christian theology.

2. "Eudaimonia"—Ideas of Happiness in Ancient Greek Philosophy

The question of human happiness was seen as a central issue in the philosophy of ancient Greece. What constitutes happiness, and how it can be attained, were much-discussed issues. Socrates, Plato, Aristotle, Epicurus and others expressed the view that man strives for happiness above all.

The Greek word for bliss is *eudaimonia*, which actually means a state of being in which the divine powers are well-disposed toward a person. In the Greek view, however, virtue is also part of happiness; a person is both happy and virtuous when his mental and physical powers are free to develop unhindered and when he brings joy to himself and to others in the general exercise of those powers. This brings a person the high regard of his contemporaries and renown in the memory of future generations. Frequently, however, such happiness is characterized by a lack of bodily needs; the fewer the sensual requirements, the greater the tranquility and satisfaction.[1]

In any event, this concept of happiness ultimately revolves around gaining the approval of the gods or of some fate-determining *daimonion*. This brings us close to that which Guggenbühl juxtaposes to "well-being," that is, the idea of "salvation."[2] I prefer to work with less "loaded" terms, since I do not want to seem like a preacher of any particular path to salvation. But the

[1]See, for example, *Dictionary of Philosophy and Religion* (William Reese, ed., New Jersey: Humanities Press, 1980), under "Eudaimonism."
[2]Guggenbühl-Craig, *Marriage—Dead or Alive*, pp. 20ff.

symbol of Paradise was originally also linked to an expectation of salvation, which lends it yet another dimension.

To the ancient Greeks, then, happiness was something approaching our modern concept of self-realization or individuation ("The greatest joy of humankind is the personality" as Goethe put it in his "West-Eastern Divan"). Self-realization is certainly a goal worth striving for, since "he who ever strives" wins the approval of the gods. The idea that the most profound happiness is ultimately to be found only in "God's love" is an important doctrine in many religions.

3. Medieval Concepts of the Earthly Paradise

The idea of a Paradise-on-earth inspired both the Latin and vernacular literatures of the Middle Ages, which contained a great variety of colorful legends about adventurous journeys to one Paradise or another. Prominent among them was the so-called Alexander saga.

Alexander the Great was alleged to have traveled to the ends of the earth and right to the gates of Paradise. In these tales, which were widespread during the Middle Ages, Paradise was described as a magical garden far to the East. The second part of an early medieval document known as the "Cosmographia," ascribed to Aethicus of Istria, consists of a kind of journal of a trip to Paradise and uses many elements from the Alexander saga.[1]

Also very popular was the legend of St. Brandanus (Brendan or Brandon), which appeared as a story in ninth-century Ireland and, so modern scholars believe, consisted of Celtic sailors' tales transferred to the person of the Irish abbot Brendan who had died some three centuries earlier, in about 577.[2] The legends tell of how Brendan decides to visit Paradise, wanders the high seas for nine years with his companions experiencing many adventures, until he finally finds the "wonderful island to the west"— and dies shortly after returning to his Irish home.

[1]Grimm, *Paradisus coelestis, Paradisus terrestris* (Celestial Paradise, Earthly Paradise), p. 103.
[2]H. Brunner, *Die poetische Insel* (The Poetic Island). Stuttgart: Metzlersche Verlagsbuchhandlung, 1967, p. 31.

This legend was incorporated into the "Lucidarius," a kind of encyclopedia of secular and religious knowledge which was regarded as one of the most important texts of the High Middle Ages. Everything contained in the "Ludicarius" was thought to be scientifically precise and true. The facticity of St. Brendan's trip to Paradise was accepted simply because it was attached to his venerated name. "Brendan's Isle," an earthly Paradise, actually appeared on world maps of that time, and from the Late Middle Ages onward numerous voyages of discovery were launched in search of such a place—the last one in 1721.[3]

In fact, such legends provided enormous impetus during the Age of Discovery, with notions about paradisial islands at the ends of the earth reinforced by travel reports from such as Columbus and Amerigo Vespucci. Cruising near the mouth of the Orinoco River, Columbus himself believed on the basis of climatic observations that he was somewhere near the earthly Paradise, "to which no one can attain, unless it be by the will of God."[4]

In general, during the Middle Ages people imagined Paradise to be somewhere on earth, picturing it sometimes as an island, sometimes as a garden to the East, sometimes on a mountain reaching to the sky. As a garden it was thought to be surrounded by a wall of jewels or of precious metals, or sometimes a wall of fire. It was described as a closed city or citadel, replete with towers and gates (see Fig. 6), sealed off from the rest of the world by dark, forested, terror-filled areas or inaccessible, snake-infested mountains.[5]

Thus the earthly Paradise, too, is inaccessible, removed from the tyranny of man, and so is imbued with a religious dimension.

Perhaps the lure of an image of Paradise may be differentiated depending on whether it relates to the earthly or the heavenly. The heavenly Paradise is promised to those who live humbly, believe in the Redeemer, and are filled with love of their neighbor and purity of heart. The earthly Paradise opens its gates—but again, only with the aid of God's will—to the courageous, active explorer of previously unknown worldly realms.

[3]Ibid., p. 32.
[4]Ibid., p. 58
[5]Bächtold-Stäubli, *Handwörterbuch des deutschen Aberglaubens* (Handbook of German Superstition).

6. Paradise as a Walled City, with the Tree of Life in the middle. A miniature
from the Floridus Book 1120, St. Bavo Cathedral, Gent.

The images of a future Paradise cited earlier from Isaiah 41 and Ezekiel 36, in which the desert is transformed into a flourishing garden through irrigation and the repopulation and rebuilding of its cities, would appear to be at the root of the pioneering spirit which gave rise to the modern state of Israel. Behind it is the perception of a "divine" task, which in the case of nonreligious people can easily take on secularized forms, such as the ideal of creating a more just world. To strictly Orthodox Jews, however, waiting for the coming of the Messiah who will open the gates of Paradise remains an article of faith, and some are therefore opposed on religious grounds to the activism involved in creating a Jewish state and physically rebuilding Zion.

But whether localized in the earthly or the heavenly realm, the basic concept of Paradise is always linked to the religious dimension, a vision of participation in divine bliss.

In the realm of modern psychology it was C. G. Jung who first saw the significance of religious ideas, examined their psychological meaning and pointed out that they can have an unconscious effect on the psyche of even presumably modern, secularized individuals. The various descriptions of Paradise as the center from which four rivers flow, the site of the Tree of Life and the Tree of Knowledge, would seem to justify the psychological interpretation that what is involved is a set of symbols for the "self."

The oscillation between images of an earthly and a heavenly Paradise, and the attendant fluctuation between a call to a contemplative and to a more active mode of "serving God," to introversion or extraversion, to a symbolic or a literal mode of comprehension—all of this, in psychological terms, reflects the constellation of the "self," a word Jung used in an attempt to illuminate certain central categories of psychic experience which we shall now briefly examine.

4. The Self in the Psychology of C. G. Jung

Up to this point, and quite in keeping with Jung's ideas, we have interpreted Paradise as an image symbolic of shelter and security within the embracing, supporting, nurturing Maternal. It represents a longing for the unitary reality which precedes the development of each individual consciousness. At the deepest level, however, the image of Paradise—precisely in its aspect as an experience of unitary reality—symbolizes what Jung himself called the "self."

Jung sees the self as the center of the total personality, which embraces both the conscious and the unconscious. "It expresses the unity of the personality as a whole."[1] The ego, on the other hand, Jung regards as "the center of my field of consciousness,"[2] while consciousness is "the function or activity which maintains the relation of psychic contents to the ego."[3] As the "subject" of the entire psyche, including the unconscious, the self is far more extensive than, and supraordinate to, the ego as the center of consciousness alone.

As a specialized term used in Analytical Psychology, then, the *self* is something highly complex and extensive. It is only partially covered by what we normally mean when we speak of self-pity, self-confidence, etc. Since they are somewhat broader in their meaning, such expressions as self-experience or self-realization more closely approximate the Jungian use of the word.

[1]*Collected Works,* Vol. 6, p. 460.
[2]Ibid., p. 425.
[3]Ibid., p. 422.

The term *self* was introduced into Freudian psychoanalysis by H. Hartmann,[4] who used it to mean the total person of a particular individual; understood as the total person, the "self" is differentiated from the "objects" of that person's environment.

Seen as a psychosomatic unit, my self embraces everything that is part of my person. Moreover, we humans develop images and valuations of ourselves. Do I like myself? Do I dislike myself? We carry around within us "representations" of ourselves which greatly influence our being and our actions. Self-confidence generally serves as the basis for spontaneous, unconstrained action, whereas self-doubt usually brings with it an involuntary calling-into-question of one's self-esteem. The images that revolve around the self as understood in these terms are of great significance for psychic well-being or malaise; representing the problems of self-image and self-valuation, they play a central role in many psychotherapies.

But C. G. Jung's use of the term "self" involves something far more extensive. When we speak of experiencing oneself or finding oneself, we clearly imply that our consciousness (with the ego as its center) wants to, or could, experience and learn something from the self. That is, the self would seem to have dimensions that can be perceived only through experiential observing of oneself, through differentiated and continuous introspection. What I know of myself is never all that I am in my entirety. We are much more than we know about ourselves. We believe that we know ourselves, yet in many situations we find that we are a mystery to our own awareness.

In any case, that which we term the self is there long before we know anything about our existence. The infant is a living self, although its ego as the center of its consciousness has not yet awakened. An archetypal predisposition to live, to satisfy the essential needs and to undergo species-appropriate development, bears witness to the effectiveness of the self in the preconscious state.

Something directs and controls bio-psychic development in accordance with certain developmental "laws" which we are now in a position to investigate. Today we can make use of the natural

[4]H. Hartmann, *Ich-Psychologie* (Ego Psychology). Stuttgart: Klett, 1972, pp. 157–180.

sciences to demonstrate how human development proceeds in the body and to localize those centers which regulate growth. We have penetrated rather far into the laws of nature. But in so doing we simply learn more and more about *how* nature functions. We still do not know *what* nature is, what life is in the full range of its physical, mental and spiritual phenomena. Nor do we know what the ultimate central authority is which regulates physical and emotional development. And yet there is a primal human urge within us to *want* to know all of this.

Everything we can investigate and comprehend involves only the *how* of that central regulation. Life and the psyche remain, at bottom, a mystery. The human need to make sense out of phenomena has caused us to ascribe names to the mysteries, names which in turn express certain symbolic concepts. For example, there is the widespread idea of a divine power which creates and guides all of life. It should be remarked at this point that it would exceed the bounds of a scientific psychology to try and deal with the question of whether God actually exists and creates the mysterious conditions of life. Psychology is concerned only with the fact that "the Divine" is evidently a symbolic idea of central importance, spontaneously produced in the human psyche, and that religious people of all periods have perceived the workings of the Divine in and around them. This idea has changed form in the course of the ages, differs from culture to culture and has been shaped to accommodate various collective forms of worship.

But whether we choose to call this central power, which is behind all physical and psychic life and their development, the gods, or the Judeo-Christian God, the idea of the Good, the metaphysical Ground of All Being, the Transcendent, or, in Jung's terms, the self—any or all of these terms point to something essentially intangible and unprovable, which nonetheless can have powerful experiential reality.

As soon as we speak of experiential reality, however, we mean reality as it impinges upon the human psyche. Transcendence is a concept which can have an effect upon us, and concepts or ideas are psychic phenomena. Since ego-consciousness is just a part of the entirety of the self, so that the self always far exceeds (transcends) the conscious ego, the self can never be fully grasped by consciousness. Hence consciousness can never prove the existence of the self.

The self can be perceived only by its effects, which for the most part manifest themselves in symbolic form. The word "symbol" derives from the Greek verb *symballein*, which literally means "to throw together." A symbol is thus something "thrown together" or composed of at least two segments or levels or areas. In the German language the word often used for it is *Sinnbild*, which is itself composed of two segments, *Bild* (image) and *Sinn* (sense or meaning)—i.e., an image in which there glimmers the hint of some deeper meaning. Every religion has its symbols, which clothe the effects of an invisible transcendent world in necessarily plastic form while at the same time pointing to a metaphysical dimension. The symbol has a uniting function, serving as a bridge between the "other world" and this world, between the sacred and the profane or, in psychological terms, between the unconscious and the conscious. It appeals to the complete range of human experience, not only to the rational faculty.[5]

The self, then, is on the one hand a hypothesis for the invisible power which is a condition of our developing consciousness and which controls or guides our total personality. It is the invisible, central, ordering factor in the human psyche. On the other hand, the self is a term for a rich vein of spontaneous symbolism which has expressive and experiential value in the human psyche.

The complexity of these ideas may become more readily comprehensible through the use of religious terminology: God has created each child as it is, giving it its inherent (or genetic) predispositions and potentialities. God then proceeds to guide the development of the child's life, which may also be viewed as its God-given destiny. Thus God's rule is made manifest in the development/destiny of the child; its bio-psychic life is ordered by that Higher Authority.

At the same time God is also a concept which is expressed in symbolic form, since the Deity itself—assuming its existence— can never be perceived by mankind in its true form. Hence a person experiences God's causality existentially, through the perception of inner forces in himself and also of limitations which he has

[5]Elaboration of the Jungian view of symbols is to be found in J. Jacobi's *Complex, Archetype, Symbol.*

not imposed upon himself but which nonetheless play an important role in molding his destiny; at the same time, some concept or image of the Divine spontaneously imprints itself upon his psyche. The mysterious "divine spark" is at work within him, and at the same time causes him to generate some idea about God and his works, an idea or image which is necessarily of a symbolic nature.

In the last two paragraphs we have used the language of religion in order to illustrate a set of complex ideas. C. G. Jung, of course, was a psychologist rather than a theologian. In using the word "self" to designate a central power or authority which guides the development of life and consciousness and at the same time constellates symbolic concepts and imagery, Jung found a neutral, psychological term which does not presuppose any particular religious inclinations. But he discovered that the self cannot be differentiated from the image of God in the human psyche, that self and God-image (*not* the Deity itself!) are identical. Wherever Jung writes of God, he always means the effects of the God-image in man, the image of the Divine in the human psyche.

Scientifically speaking, the self is a hypothesis of a central, invisible, ordering factor in our life and experience. It is our predisposition to develop concepts and images, and thus to evolve an ego-consciousness which enjoys relative freedom and autonomy. We could therefore virtually define the self as "the inherent potentiality of becoming human." It is precisely this mystery of the inherent potentiality as the origin of everything human, everything conscious (for without consciousness humanity cannot experience itself as human, the world does not exist for it at all), which constellates the previously mentioned fantasy image of a primal, paradisial, unitary reality.

Jung has also referred to the self as the *coincidentia oppositorum*, the uniting of opposites. Consciousness is inconceivable without polarities, though these also rend us and plunge us into conflict. When the polarities are united there is harmony and peace, the soul becomes a single entity which embraces and unites all opposites. Balance, peace, harmony—these constitute a wish-fulfillment image, a goal, which has exerted a powerful attraction for people in all times and which stands in crass opposition to the conflict-laden reality of human existence. It is behind revolutionary ideas from the French Revolution through Marx to Marcuse.

And so it would seem that mankind has never really accepted the loss of Paradise. Whether localized in this world or the next, images of Paradise have always attracted a great deal of psychic energy. Release from the burden of existence, from the sometimes unbearable tension of opposites, is a main concern of many religions. In contrast to Freud, who tried to demonstrate that religious ideas are mere infantilism, Jung took the psychological importance of such ideas and images very seriously. In my view it was one of Jung's major accomplishments to have founded a new psychology of religion which delineates the significance of religious experience in the psychic realm. If Paradise as "God's garden" is part of the symbolism of the self, then it cannot be enough to interpret every paradisial image regressively. Such symbolism relates to both the beginning and the end of the process of individuation or self-realization.

A central symbol of the self as wholeness is the circle (see Fig. 7). As the most perfect shapes, the sphere and circle symbolized Existence in the ancient world, or the Divine according to Plotinus. The rolling wheel was a representation of God common in medieval mysticism. Nicolaus Cusanus imagined the Deity as a circle with an infinite radius. The circle motif coupled with the square is commonly found in Far Eastern mandalas designed to serve the purposes of meditation.

There are also medieval mandalas with Christ at the center, surrounded by the four Evangelists. The "squaring of the circle" has fascinated countless generations of scholars, who saw in it an important mystery. And Neumann has written: "The symbol of the circular mandala stands at the beginning as at the end. In the beginning it takes the mythological form of paradise; in the end, of the Heavenly Jerusalem."[6] Jung, too, saw parallels between Paradise and the Heavenly Jerusalem.

Paradise is another term for the "Kingdom of Heaven." An important element in the Christian conception of the Heavenly Kingdom is that it is eternal. We come from there, have a limited

[6]*The Origins and History of Consciousness*, Part I, p. 37.

PARADISUS TERRESTRIS

7. *The Creation of the World.*
Woodcut in Jacobus Philippus Bergamensis' *Supplementum
Chronicarum,* Venice, 1486.

temporal existence here in the world, and return (under certain conditions) whence we have come. But there are conditions imposed on that return. Something should—and must—be done here in the temporal realm. Demands are made for a certain attitude of consciousness, goals established of an ethical nature as well.

Thus man experiences himself or herself as a creature to which an objective has been given, something that must be attained or fulfilled. This means that a human being cannot wait passively for redemption from the state of conflict; he must do something active to bring it about. Psychologically it might be said that the self gives the ego an assignment, a task to be performed.

5. Paradise and the Process of Individuation

It is, in any case, a specifically human trait to feel oneself oriented toward the image of some goal or objective. Man must be in the world for some purpose; there must be some ideas or images that have sufficient quality of summons or challenge, that transmit to man some glimmer of life's meaning and purpose. That is humanity's specific situation in the cosmos. A human being must pursue a goal-oriented course which seems meaningful somehow. Depressive and suicide-prone individuals generally remark that life has no meaning for them. The loss of a possible meaning which transcends life-for-its-own-sake has a catastrophic effect on the human psyche.

The ancient Chinese saw the ultimate purpose of man as "being in Tao." *Tao* means not only goal, but also way or path, and meaning. Being on the proper path is thus at one and the same time the meaning and the goal of human life. Man must fight the dragon in order to gain the "treasure difficult to attain," must search for the Philospher's Stone or distill it out of base matter, must *earn* the Kingdom of Heaven, the state of harmony. In brief, a human being must go beyond purely "natural" existence, carry out some special task. It is only in executing his (or her) particular task that he becomes that which he really is and truly realizes himself. As Jung writes:

> In the last analysis every life is the realization of a whole, that is, of a self, for which reason this realization can also be called "individuation." All life is bound to individual carriers who realize it, and it is simply inconceivable without them. But every carrier is

202

charged with an individual destiny and destination, and the realization of these alone makes sense of life.[1]

The poet Bergengrün had something similar in mind when he wrote that the important thing is "to take the design that Destiny has for you and make it your own."

A dream drawn from my practice may help to illustrate how the self can be experienced as an authority which transmits the sense of task and destiny. The dream is that of a young man whose professional aim was to become a Jungian analyst: "It was after my death. I was finally free of earth, free to glide through the heights and depths, liberated from all gravity. It was a magnificent sensation. I saw the earth from afar. Suddenly my activity came to a halt. A man appeared and handed out assignments. Mine was emblazoned on the heavens. I had to bring the number seven to mankind. I knew that the task would be extremely difficult and burdensome, but that there was no escaping it."

The dreamer was a young man who was fascinated by everything unusual, including the irrational aspect of Jungian psychology and his own experience of the unconscious. He was a master at evading matters related to "earth's gravity," the banalities of everyday life and its monotonous, boring effortfulness, in order to concern himself with "higher" things such as Zen Buddhism, the psychology of religion, etc.

But everyday things had a way of creeping up on him from behind: he kept running out of money because he couldn't be bothered to budget it; he was constantly in need of sleep because he spent days and nights discussing God and the nature of the world, and so he didn't have enough time for study and work. Most of his books were only half-read, because by midpoint his interest had already shifted to something new. And he imagined that the analytical profession must be incredibly interesting and fascinating, since one functioned in a world of dreams and fantasies. He could think of nothing he wanted more than to have such an occupation himself.

Apparently he believed that such a choice would enable him to legitimately float free of the "gravity" which so oppressed and bored him. But that, of course, would also have meant the end

[1]*Collected Works*, Vol. 12, p. 222.

of his earthly existence, his effectiveness as a social being. More-over at that point he would never have been able to stick it out "through thick and thin" and simply *be there* for other people —which is an absolute necessity in the psychotherapeutic profession. On the other hand, he had an extremely subtle comprehension of psychic reality and was highly gifted in matters psychological.

His motivation for choosing the profession of analyst had always seemed to me extremely dubious. Now this dream came and stated that his "floating around" had to come to an end. He could not ultimately escape the responsibility of truly developing his talent and placing it at society's disposal. This he was commanded to do from "cosmic space," by a man who certainly represented a supraordinate psychic authority and thus may be regarded as a symbol of the self. His assigned task appeared in the sky, emblazoned in letters of light—i.e., it had an illuminating quality, it "enlightened" consciousness.

The dreamer's task is to bring the number seven to the people of earth. Seven has always been regarded as an important, sacred number. The period during which God created the world was seven days—which is why the week is thus divided. The Babylonian creation myth *Enuma Elish* was written out on seven tablets, also underscoring the creative significance of the number seven. In ancient times there were thought to be seven planets and seven metals. In Western music our basic scale consists of seven tones, the seventh being the so-called leading tone, which strives to move to the eighth (octave) tone in order for the scale to attain completion. According to H. von Beit, the number seven is frequently linked to an image of the soul.[2] In all these contexts it is connected to the idea of a sequence, a cycle, a return and thus a rebirth. In contrast to the static numerals four or eight, which are regarded as symbols of wholeness, seven is dynamic, not yet complete—as is so aptly exemplified in the diatonic scale. As Jung has said: "The seven stages symbolize the transformation."[3]

The numeral seven, then, is linked to psychic transformation,

[2]H. Von Beit, *Symbolik des Marchens* (The Symbolism of Fairytales). Berne: Francke, 1960, p. 258.
[3]*Collected Works*, Vol. 12, p. 76.

that is, to the constant process of self-becoming, which strives for completeness but attains it only to perceive it as a transition to a new stage of becoming. If the dreamer is told that he must bring this number to mankind, this means that he must first integrate it into himself before he will be capable of passing it along to others. Hence he must first dedicate himself to more profound work on his own psychic development. That development, at the same time, implies a level of social responsibility concomitant with its own depths.

This dream can indeed be seen as a portrait of an inner call to a vocation. Many other dreams pointed in that same direction. Since experiencing them the dreamer has come far along the path to becoming an excellent analyst. In the process he has gained considerably in ego-strength, a sense of reality and responsibility, and has developed his own particular abilities more highly.

On a more general level the question might be raised at this point as to what extent the process of individuation dealt with in Analytical Psychology may be regarded as a way to regain Paradise, and thus as a "doctrine of salvation." Many young people have come to the C. G. Jung Institute in Zurich over the years in the hopes of experiencing a satisfying "Jungian trip"—perhaps as a substitute for a pilgrimage to India. It strikes me that the attraction of Jungian ideas often is based on such expectations. I remember, for example, a prominent industrial official who came to me in the expectation of "immersing himself in myth through analysis," as he expressed it. His hope-filled idea was that one need only plunge into the mythic depths and existence would be transfigured into a kind of Paradise—psychic deep-sea diving, as it were.

In this context it is interesting to note the idea prevalent in some archaic societies that, by means of certain ecstatic techniques, the shaman or medicine man can establish a link to the lost Paradise. This appears to be the essence of his healing power. According to some archaic beliefs, during his initiation the shaman encounters an animal that reveals to him certain secrets of his vocation, teaches him the language of the animals or becomes his helpful spirit-guide. Friendship with the animals and knowledge of their language constitute a paradisial condition, since according to many primitive beliefs the animals "know the secrets of Life and Nature, they even know the secrets of longevity and immortality."[4]

Using ecstatic techniques the shaman can also undertake a journey to heaven; he can leave his mortal body and travel to the upper or the lower realms. The important thing is that the shaman's trip to heaven uses the medium of a tree or a post. He may, for example, climb a birch trunk which serves as a tent-pole but is also symbolic of the cosmic tree which stands at the center of the world and from whose crown the North Star shines.

> By ascending it [the pole in the middle of the yurt] the candidate enters into Heaven; that is why, as soon as he comes out of the smoke-hole of the tent he gives a loud cry, invoking the help of the gods: up there, he finds himself in their presence . . . . To sum up: the most representative mystical experience of the archaic societies, that of shamanism, betrays the *Nostalgia for Paradise*, the desire to recover the state of freedom and beatitude before "the Fall," the will to restore communication between Earth and Heaven . . . .[5]

It seems to me that there is an obvious similarity between my analysand's dream and these ideas about the tasks and abilities of the archaic shaman. The latter's mystical journey is highly reminiscent of the joyous, gravity-free soaring in the dream discussed earlier.

It would seem to be in keeping with archetypal expectations when physicians and psychotherapists are seen as healers who, being themselves in contact with "Paradise," have the power to redeem people from suffering, tension and illness and thus to open the pathway to paradisial happiness. Such a hope is in fact unconsciously present in many people when despair drives them to seek the aid of a psychotherapist. To what extent there is a predominance of regressive need for paradisial security through merging with the positive, maternal analyst, and to what extent a recognition that the therapist's help is primarily a means to redemptive self-discovery, depends on the individual's psychic maturity.

[4]Mircea Eliade, *Myths, Dreams and Mysteries*. Harper Torchbooks. New York: Harper & Bros., 1960, p. 63.
[5]Ibid., pp. 64, 66.

In practice it is not always possible to neatly differentiate between the search for the self in infantile unitary reality and the same search as the goal of expanding consciousness; the two are frequently intertwined. Jung rightfully saw regression as not always something pathological, but often a *reculer pour mieux sauter*. Especially in cases involving a disturbed primal relationship, a certain gap in attention and acceptance must first be filled in through the experience of the transference before the "path of individuation" can be followed; in this sense the process of self-realization may be seen as the moving force behind regressive needs.

Mircea Eliade points out that Christianity is dominated by the longing for Paradise. He states: ". . . paradisiac symbolism is attested in the rites of baptism," and goes on to quote J. Danielou: "Instead of Adam falling under the domination of Satan and being expelled from Paradise, the catechumen appears as though set free by the New Adam from the power of Satan and re-admitted into Paradise" (*Bible et Liturgie*, Paris, 1951, p. 46).

Quoting other sources, Eliade continues:

> Christianity thus seems to be the realization of Paradise. The Christ is the Tree of Life (Ambrose, *De Isaac*, 5, 43) or the Fountain of Paradise (Ambrose, *De Paradiso*, III, 272, 10). But this realization of Paradise takes place in three successive phases. Baptism is the entry into Paradise . . . the mystical life is a deeper entry into Paradise . . . and finally, death introduces the martyrs into Paradise. . . . it is remarkable indeed to have found the paradisiac language applied to all three aspects of the Christian life.[6]

However, although Christianity may be strongly permeated by the longing for Paradise, in the final analysis it is only the mystics who achieve a partial restoration of the paradisial condition: friendship with the animals (e.g., Francis of Assisi), ascension to Heaven, encounter with God. Psychologically the reference is to an intensive encounter with the inner world and its center, the self, which can generate an experience of the most intense numinosity.[7]

[6]Ibid., p. 67.
[7]Rudolf Otto, *The Idea of the Holy*. New York: Oxford University Press, reprinted 1972.

Feelings of longing for Paradise and images of "true happiness" can, of course, vary greatly, depending on such factors as emotional maturity, religious or philosophical orientation, etc. But in any case the self, as expressed for instance in the image of Paradise as a symbol of the true center, is not necessarily identical with what is commonly called "happiness." In prosaic everyday terms, the self would seem rather to be an inner psychic possibility of integrating various conflicting reaction patterns and tendencies within the individual personality.

The circle is an eloquent symbol for the practical processes involved in such integration. When, for example, we circumambulate conflicted contents through reflection or meditation, we often find a variety of approaches to the same problem rising into consciousness. Psychologically speaking, that brings about a certain relativization of the ego standpoint and yields the experience of greater flexibility and freedom. This makes it possible to at least partially disengage from total identification with particular conflicts, desires and fears. The ego may then shift its stance and gain a new orientation. This does not mean that a particular problem has been eliminated, but perhaps new strength has thus been found to bear it and deal with it sensibly.

The other-worldly aspect of such symbolism as Paradise or the Heavenly Jerusalem seems to point to the inherent human capacity to distance oneself from one's own ego, to go down into the depths, to sense one's rootedness in suprapersonal dimensions of meaning. The Tree of Life, the Tree of Knowledge and the four rivers no doubt symbolize the fact that such experiences can creatively give rise to new attitudes and deeper insights which can reorient a person's life or set it flowing once again.

All of the above is a purely formal effort to circumambulate processes which are virtually indescribable, but which in practice are generally of a religious or philosophical nature, since the search for meaning is of their essence.

In 1937 Jung wrote:

No matter what the world thinks about religious experience, the one who has it possesses a great treasure, a thing that has become for him a source of life, meaning and beauty, and that has given a new splendour to the world and to mankind. He has *pistis* and peace . . . Is there, as a matter of fact, any better truth about the ultimate things than the one that helps you to live?[8]

Aniela Jaffé rightly states that Jung never again expressed himself so positively on this point, since even the experience of the numinous cannot guarantee inner peace, certainly not over the long haul. She writes:

> So long as one continues to develop, inner peace, even for those whose life has been enriched by an encounter with the unconscious, is only a breathing-space between the conflict solved and the conflict to come, between answers and questions that throw us into turmoil and suffering, until new insights or new transformations bring a fresh solution and the inner and outer opposites are once again reconciled.[9]

It would appear that Jung himself at times became overly enthusiastic about the idea of inner peace, carried away with a belief in the possibility of existence in one's own inner psychic Paradise. But that possibility, so the Bible tells us, is barred by the "flaming sword which turns every way."

The symbolism of Paradise can thus be seen both in regressive and in prospective terms. In the case of the analysand mentioned earlier (cf. p. 106), in whose dream the gate of Paradise opened, the emphasis was on a regressive longing to merge with the positive-maternal. This is doubtless why he did not enter the Paradise with the peaceful animals in his dream. Instead there was a counter-movement, in the form of a fear that this Paradise could mean death, i.e., the wiping out of autonomous ego-consciousness.

But how are we to understand the following dream of a 45-year-old woman?

There has been a murder. The dreamer wishes to avoid this event by entering the forest. She asks herself whether she is guilty of the murder and then sees the severed head of a girl lying on the ground. She goes deep into the woods and makes herself comfortable under branches and undergrowth. Now peaceful animals come to her. She recalls most vividly that fox and hare are

---

[8]*Collected Works*, Vol. 11, p. 105.
[9]Jaffé, *The Myth of Meaning*, pp. 55–56.

together. All of this makes her feel very good. On waking, she has the feeling that she had visited a paradisial place in her dream.

Without going into details here, we are certainly faced with the question of whether this forest episode is to be interpreted only as flight, as an escape from the murderous decapitation to a back-to-nature image of peace and harmony. But the fact that the fox and the hare came to her in peaceable unity had a numinous quality for the dreamer. A higher power must have intervened, since fox and hare do not normally live in peace with one another; something has been united here which cannot generally be united in nature.

In a state of inner fragmentation, symbolized by the decapitation motif, the dreamer finds her way inside herself to a place of miraculous "unitary reality." She becomes a kind of hermit and experiences her own unity with nature. The place is very remote from the everyday world; it is that place, in the words of an old German adage, "where fox and hare say goodnight to each other." That place of peace between fox and hare does not exist on this earth, of course, which lends a dimension of mystery and profundity to the old saying. And the fact that in her dream, the hare need have no fear of the fox, is of special relevance to the dreamer, since her chief symptoms involve neurotic anxiety.

It seems to me that the discovery of this inner place where harmony and trust predominate may depict an important event in the dreamer's own individuation process. To use a term introduced by Neumann, it would involve awareness of the ego-self axis, an "experience of the harmony of the individual ego with the totality of its nature, with its constitutional make-up."[10] It is an empirical fact in therapy that experience of this ego-self axis can provide an existential sense of greater depth and renewed energy, that as an experience of meaning it is generally accompanied by genuine gratification and so, in a profound sense, can bring "happiness."

The question remains of what implications at the level of social psychology may be involved in such striving for individuation and self-affirmation. The dream just cited might seem to suggest that flight from the world to an inner place of possible harmony is an inevitable concomitant. In contrast to that, however, there is the

[10] *The Child*, p. 43.

dream previously cited in which a young man is given an assignment by "higher authority" to bring the number seven to mankind. The ancient Greeks regarded it as very important that the untrammeled development of the individual's mental and physical forces also benefit others, i.e., that self-realization always maintain a social context as well.

At this point I should like to reiterate Jung's statement that "individuation means precisely the better and more complete fulfillment of the collective qualities of the human being, since adequate consideration of the peculiarity of the individual is more conducive to a better social performance than when the peculiarity is neglected or suppressed."[11] The process of individuation can take place only in a context of interpersonal, societal and cultural relationships. Self-realization always includes expending oneself for suprapersonal goals, in accordance with one's own conscience and best knowledge. And that "conscience and best knowledge," which functions as the decisionmaking authority within whatever larger context one is operating in, is likewise an expression of the self, involving rootedness in the vertical dimension.

[11]*Collected Works*, Vol. 7, p. 174.

6. Summing Up

In conclusion we may say that conflicts, external or internal, are always with us, that they are in fact a condition of human maturation in the individuation process. Thus the essence of all images of Paradise is the need to provide an explanation for the fact of this earthly "vale of tears" and human vulnerability. From this perspective the condition of human suffering arises through separation from an original place and condition of conflict-free bliss, caused by human guilt. On the basis of this archetypal concept, it would seem that the myth of Paradise provides three focal points around which imagination, thought and striving revolve.

The first focal point involves the locale and condition of bliss. It provides the impetus for a broad spectrum of fantasies and wishful thinking, described in more or less familiar terms of a past (and lost) or future Paradise. The specifics may involve a Golden Age, the Blessed Isles, a desert island *à la* Robinson Crusoe or a version of the Lotus Land fantasy (the latter, which frequently involve details of endless food provided with no effort, of sausages growing on fences or broiled squab which fly right into the mouths of indolent though fortunate humans, are generally categorized by scholars among the "liars' tales").[1]

Since the days of Sir Thomas More we also have the social utopias as fabricated counter-images to existing conditions. Such a utopian situation does not exist anywhere in this world, of

[1]See, for example, Boltke and Polivka, *Anmerkungen zu den Kinder- und Hausmärchen der Brüder Grimm* (Notes on the Fairytales of the Brothers Grimm), Vol. 3. Hildesheim: Olms, 1963.

8. *The Garden of Eden as a Sphere.*
From the Book of Hours, *Very Rich Hours,* created for the
Duke de Berry (1340-1416).

course, but it *could* exist.[2] (The "negative utopias" developed by
such writers as Aldous Huxley and George Orwell are a phenomenon of the 20th century, in which faith in social and technological progress has been severely shaken.) The potentially explosive
power of social utopias, even today, is a subject which hardly
needs elaboration here.

These days, of course, travel agents offer us all manner of
"vacation paradise," shopping centers promise us a "consumer's
paradise," nudist camps call themselves "sunbather's paradise,"
Communist countries bill themselves as "workers' paradise." And
on the individual level Paradise can present itself as the specific
image of whatever seems to promise the fulfillment of the most
urgent wishes or drives—especially those which cannot be realized in this world. For example, there may be the narcissistic wish
to be loved and admired as a great genius. The ideal of the "good
life" may resolve itself into the fantasy of owning a castle in Pro-
vence, of making love to the world's most beautiful women on
a tropical island, or merely of driving a priceless Ferrari racing car.
Of course, such paradisial images often are symptomatic in
character, masking more genuine or deeply hidden needs for
unity within oneself, needs which for various reasons can find no
more adequate means of expression.

The second focal point derived from the myth of Paradise is
based on sadness at the loss of Paradise and consideration of how
the painful separation from the original place and condition of
bliss came about. Most myths assume that the cause of the separation was some form of human guilt or "sin." Yet even in an early
Easter liturgy Adam's fall from grace is described as a "felix
culpa," a "felicitous guilt," since without Original Sin mankind
would not have stood in need of redemption and therefore salvation would not have arrived in the form of God's incarnation.

The same liturgical passage states that the *peccatum* (sin) was
certe necessarium (surely necessary). In Milton's epic work
"Paradise Lost" (1667), too, mankind's sin is ameliorated and its
dignity magnified, in that before expulsion from the garden God
shows Adam the path leading to redemption.

---

[2]The word "utopia" comes from the Greek *ou* (not) and *topos* (place); the idea
of "nowhere" was taken up by Samuel Butler in his famous satirical work
Erewhon, the title of which is simply "nowhere" turned backwards.

The philosophy of the Enlightenment brought new interpretations of the Fall. Kant regarded it as an extremely important developmental step in history, a reaching out for human maturity. Thus, for Kant, the post-paradisial condition constituted a kind of coming-of-age. Schiller, to whom man's alleged disobedience to the divine commandment was a "defection from instinct," formulated his ideas as follows:

> This defection of mankind from instinct, which brought moral evil into Creation but only for the purpose of making moral good possible there, is without doubt the most fortunate, the greatest event in human history; humanity's freedom dates from that instant, the laying of the first remote foundation-stone of its morality . . . Man turned from an innocent creature into a guilty one, from a perfect ward of nature into an imperfect moral being, from a happy instrument into an unhappy artist.[3]

The third point of emphasis is the longing for a place or condition of bliss and the desire to close the gap which separates one from it. Ultimately this is the source of all expectations of salvation and redemption, whether played out in the religious, mystical, secular or even banal realm.

The "longing for Paradise" may assume the most familiar and the most unlikely forms, may reveal itself in the most sublime manner or mask itself behind the most abstruse activities. It can be progressive or regressive; it can lend impetus to the search for the deepest secrets of the cosmos, but in the form of a fanatical drive to reshape the world as a utopia it can also turn brutally dangerous. It reveals itself behind a vast range of emotional disturbances, including the urge to suicide ("No one can help me in *this* world!"), but also plays a decisive role in the process of human maturation, self-realization or individuation.

It is of decisive practical importance in what form an archetypal phenomenon such as the "longing for Paradise" manifests itself and on what level it can be understood and lived out. I believe that the essential task of depth psychology must be to promote the development of consciousness, in order to make possible a differentiation of the various levels at which archetypal ideas make their impact. This is why, to the countless attempts at interpreta-

[3]F. Schiller, *Werke* (Works), Vol. 16, cited in *Die Sache mit dem Apfel* (The Business with the Apple), by J. Illies.

tion of the Paradise myth which have been made through the centuries, I have ventured to add a new effort from the standpoint of depth psychology. The best we can hope for is an approximate answer to the question of how and on what levels such a myth pattern—as an inherent, archetypal component of human experience—influences the individual and collective sense of existence today.

References

1. Bächtold-Stäubli, H., *Handwörterbuch des deutschen Aberglaubens* (Handbook of German Superstition), Berlin & Leipzig: de Gruyter, 1927–1942.
2. Balint, Michael, *Primary Love and Psycho-Analytic Technique,* New York: Liveright Publ. Corp., 1965.
3. Baumann, H., *Schöpfung und Urzeit des Menschen im Mythus der afrikanischen Völker* (Creation and the Primal Era of Mankind in the Mythology of African Peoples), Berlin: Reimer, 1936.
4. Von Beit, H., *Symbolik des Märchens* (The Symbolism of Fairytales), Berne: Francke, 1960.
5. Bettelheim, Bruno, *Children of the Dream*, New York: The Macmillan Company, 1969.
6. Bible: *The New Oxford Annotated Bible*, Revised Standard Version, New York: Oxford University Press, 1977.
7. *Biblisches Nachschlagewerk* (Biblical Reference Book), Stuttgart: Württembergische Bibelanstalt, 1964.
8. Boltke and Polivka, *Anmerkungen zu den Kinder- und Hausmärchen der Brüder Grimm* (Notes on the Fairytales of the Brothers Grimm), Vol. 3, Hildesheim: Olms, 1963.
9. Bottero, J., "Jüdiche Schöpfungsmythen" (Jewish Creation Myths), in *Quellen des alten Orients* (Sources of the Ancient Orient), Vol. I, Einsiedeln: Benziger, 1964.
10. Bruning, K. A., "Die Sache mit Eva—in der Sicht des Vorgeschichtlers" (The Business With Eve—from the Perspective of the Prehistorian), in *Die Sache mit dem Apfel* (The Business with the Apple), by J. Illies; see Ref. 39.
11. Brunner, H., *Die poetische Insel* (The Poetic Island), Stuttgart: Metzlersche Verlagsbuchhandlung, 1967.

12. Deakin, M., *The Children on the Hill*, London: 1972.

13. Eibl-Eibesfeldt, Irenaeus, *Love and Hate: The Natural History of Behavior Patterns,* New York: Holt, Rinehart & Winston, 1972.

14. Eliade, Mircea, *Myths, Dreams and Mysteries*, Harper Torchbooks, New York: Harper & Bros., 1960.

15. Erikson, Erik H., *Childhood and Society*, New York: W. W. Norton & Co., 1950.

16. Fordham, Michael, "Individuation and Ego Development," in *Journal of Analytical Psychology*, Vol. III, No. 2 (1958), London.

17. _____, *Children As Individuals,* London: Hodder & Stoughton, 1969.

18. _____, "Maturation of Ego and Self in Infancy," in *Analytical Psychology—A Modern Science* (Library of Analytical Psychology, Vol. 1), London: 1973.

19. _____, *Self and Autism* (Library of Analytical Psychology, Vol. 3), London: 1976.

20. _____, "The Self as an Imaginative Construct," in *Journal of Analytical Psychology*, Vol. 24, 1979.

21. Franz, M.-L. von, *Shadow and Evil in Fairytales*, Zurich: Spring Publications, 1974.

22. Frazer, G., *The New Golden Bough*, New York: Criterion Books, 1959.

23. Freud, Anna, *Wege und Irrwege in der Kinderentwicklung* (Pathways and Detours in Child Development), Berne: Huber; Stuttgart: Klett, 1968. Vol. 7 of "Schriften zur Psychoanalyse und psychosomatischen Medizin." Original: *Normality and Pathology in Childhood*. New York: International Universities Press.

24. Freud, Sigmund, *The Complete Psychological Works*, Standard Edition. London: Hogarth Press, 1973.

25. Gehlen, A., *Der Mensch* (The Person), Bonn, 1955.

26. Goethe, J. W. von, *Faust, Part I*; translated by Philip Wayne. Penguin Classics, Harmondsworth, Middlesex: Penguin Books, 1949.

27. Grimm, R., "Die Paradiesesehe, eine erotische Utopie des Mittelalters" (The Paradisial Marriage, a Medieval Erotic Utopia), in *Festschrift W. Mohr* (Göppinger Arbeiten zur Germanistik, 65). Göppingen: 1972.

28. _____, *Paradisus coelestis, Paradisus terrestris* (Celestial Paradise, Earthly Paradise). Munich: W. Fink Verlag, 1977.

29. Guggenbühl-Craig, Adolf, *Marriage—Dead or Alive*, Zurich: Spring Publications, 1977.

30. Gunkel, H., *Schöpfung und Chaos in Urzeit und Endzeit* (Creation and Chaos in Primal Time and at the End of Days). Göttingen: 1895.

31. _____, *Göttinger Handkommentar zum Alten Testament* (The Handy Göttingen Commentary to the Old Testament), 5th edition, Vol. I. Göttingen: 1922.

32. Haag, H. E., *Der Mensch am Anfang* (Mankind at the Beginning), Trier: Paulinus Verlag, 1970.

33. Hahn, A., *Soziologie der Paradiesvorstellungen* (The Sociology of Ideas of Paradise). Trier University Addresses, Vol. 7, Trier: 1976.

34. Hartmann, H., *Ich-Psychologie* (Ego Psychology), Stuttgart: Klett, 1972.

35. Hesiod, *Works and Days*, verses 110–120; translated by Richard Lattimore. Ann Arbor, Michigan: University of Michigan Press, 1959.

36. Höffe, O., "Herrschaftsfreiheit oder gerechte Herrschaft?" (Arbitrary Rule or a Just Rule?), in *Neue Zürcher Zeitung*, section "Zeitfragen" (Issues of the Day), July 30–31, 1977.

37. Hurwitz, E., *Otto Gross, Paradies-Sucher zwischen Freud und Jung* (Otto Gross, Paradise Seeker Between Freud and Jung), Zurich and Frankfurt: Suhrkamp, 1979.

38. Huxley, Aldous, *Brave New World*, New York: Harper and Bros., 1950.

39. Illies, J., *Die Sache mit dem Apfel* (The Business with the Apple), Freiburg im Breisgau: Herder, 1972.

40. Jacobi, Jolande, *Complex, Archetype, Symbol*, Bollingen Series LVII, New York: Pantheon Books, 1959.

41. _____, *Frauenprobleme, Eheprobleme* (Women's Problems, Marriage Problems), Zurich: Rascher, 1968.

42. Jacobsohn, H., "The Dialogue of a World-Weary Man With His Ba," in *Timeless Documents of the Soul* (part of the series "Studies from the C. G. Jung Institute, Zurich"), Evanston, Illinois: Northwestern University Press, 1968.

43. Jacoby, Mario, "Autorität und Revolte—der Mythus vom Vatermord" (Authority and Revolt—The Myth of Patricide), in *Zeitschrift für analytische Psychologie*, Vol. 6, No. 4, 1975.

44. _____, V. Kast, and I. Riedel, *Das Böse im Märchen* (Evil in Fairytales), Fellbach: Bonz, 1978.

45. Jaffé, Aniela, *The Myth of Meaning*, New York: published by Putnam's for the C. G. Jung Foundation, 1971.

46. Jung, Eberhard, "Analytische Psychologie und Rauschmittelprob-

lematik" (Analytical Psychology and Drug Problems), in *Zeitschrift für analytische Psychologie*, Vol. 6, No. 1, 1975.

47. Jung, Emma, *Animus and Anima*, New York: The Analytical Psychology Club of New York, 1957.

48. Jung, C. G. *Collected Works*, Vols. 6–8, 9 (I and II), 10–12, 17, New York: Pantheon Books, for the Bollingen Foundation.

49. Klein, Melanie, *The Psychoanalysis of Children*, New York: Dell, 1976.

50. Kohut, H., see *The Analysis of Self* (1971) and *The Restoration of the Self* (1977), both published by International University Press, New York.

51. Koliadis, E., *Mütterliche Erwerbstätigkeit und kindliche Sozialisation* (Working Mothers and the Socialization of Children), Weinheim & Basel: Beltz, 1975.

52. Lambert, S. K., "Archetypische Funktionen, Objektbeziehungen und internalisierte Objekte" (Archetypal Functions, Object Relations and Internalized Objects), in *Zeitschrift fur analytische Psychologie*, Vol. 8, No. 1, 1977.

53. Lehr, U., *Die Bedeutung der Familie im Sozialisationsprozess* (The Importance of the Family in the Socialization Process), Stuttgart: Kohlhammer, 1973.

54. Leibbrand, A. and W., *Formen des Eros* (Forms of Eros), Vol. I, Freiburg & Munich: Alber, 1972.

55. Maag, V., "Syrien—Palästina" (Syria—Palestine), in Schmökel, *Kulturgeschichte des alten Orients* (Cultural History of the Ancient Orient), Stuttgart: Kroner, 1961.

56. Mahler, M. S., *On Human Symbiosis and the Vicissitudes of Individuation*, New York: International University Press, 1968.

57. _____, *The Psychological Birth of the Human Infant: Symbiosis and Individuation*, New York: Basic Books, 1975.

58. Mause, L. de, *Hört ihr die Kinder weinen* (Hear the Children Crying), Frankfurt/M: Suhrkamp, 1977. Original: *The History of Childhood*. New York: Psychohistory Press, 1974.

59. Mead, Margaret, *Sex and Temperament in Three Primitive Societies*, New York: William Morrow & Co., 1963.

60. Menschik, J., *Feminismus* (Feminism), Cologne: Pahl-Rugenstein, 1977.

61. Meyerhofer, M., from an unpublished lecture, Zurich, c. 1967.

62. Neill, A. S., *The Free Child*, London, 1952.

63. Neumann, Erich, *The Origins and History of Consciousness*, 2 vols., New York: Harper & Bros., for the Bollingen Foundation, 1962.

64. _____, "Narcissism, Normal Self-Formation and the Primary Relation to the Mother," in *Spring* 1966, New York: The Analytical Psychology Club of New York.

65. _____, *The Great Mother*, New York: Pantheon Books, for the Bollingen Foundation, 1955.

66. _____, "Die Erfahrung der Einheitswirklichkeit" (The Experience of Unitary Reality), in *Der schöpferische Mensch* (The Creative Person), Zurich: Rhein Verlag, 1964.

67. _____, *The Child*, New York: G. P. Putnam's Sons, for the C. G. Jung Foundation, 1973.

68. _____, *Depth Psychology and a New Ethic*, New York: G. P. Putnam's Sons, for the C. G. Jung Foundation, 1969.

69. Otto, Rudolf, *The Idea of the Holy*, New York: Oxford University Press, reprinted 1972.

70a. Parin, P., F. Morgenthaler and G. Parin-Matthey, *Fear Thy Neighbor As Thyself: Psychoanalysis and Society Among the Anyi of West Africa*, Chicago: University of Chicago Press, 1980.

70b. _____, *Die Weissen denken zu viel* (White Men Think Too Much), Munich: Kindler Taschenbuch 2079 o.J.

71. *Dictionary of Philosophy and Religion*, William Reese, ed., New Jersey: Humanities Press, 1980. See entry on "Eudaimonism."

72. Portmann, A., *Zoologie und das neue Bild des Menschen* (Zoology and the New Image of Man), Hamburg: Rowohlt, 1958.

73. Renggli, F., *Angst und Geborgenheit* (Fear and Security), Reinbek: Rowohlt, 1976.

74. Ritter, P. and J., *Freie Kindererziehung in der Familie* (Free Childrearing in the Family), Reinbek: Rowohlt, 1972.

75. Robertson, J., "Mutter-Kind Interaktion im ersten Lebensjahr" (Mother-Child Interaction in the First Year of Life), *Psyche*, Vol. 2, 1977.

76. Rosenberg, A., "Das älteste Drama" (The Oldest Drama) in *Die Sache mit dem Apfel*; see Ref. 39.

77. Rousseau, J.-J., *Emile: Or, Education*, Totowa, New Jersey: Biblio Distribution Centre, 1972.

78. Schiller, F., *Werke* (Works), Vol. 16, cited in *Die Sache mit dem Apfel*; see Ref. 39.

79. Spitz, René A., *The First Year of Life*, New York: International Universities Press, 1965.

80. Sprenger, J., and H. Institoris, *Der Hexenhammer* (The "Malleus Maleficorum"), Berlin: Barsdorf Verlag, 1506.

81. Steck, O. H., *Die Paradieserzählung* (The Tale of Paradise), in the series "Biblische Studien," Neukirchener Verlag, 1970.

82. Uexküll, T., *Grundfragen der psychosomatischen Medizin* (Basic Questions of Psychosomatic Medicine), Munich: Rowohlt, 1968.
83. Webster's *Third New International Dictionary, Unabridged*, Springfield, Mass.: G. & C. Merriam, 1969.
84. Wickler, Wolfgang, *The Biology of the Ten Commandments*, New York: McGraw-Hill, 1972.
85. Widmer, S., in an article in the weekly newspaper *Züri-Leu*, Zurich, July 1979.
86. Winnicott, D. W., *The Maturational Processes and the Facilitating Environment*, New York: International University Press, 1965.

Index

223